Aztec, Salmon, and the Puebloan Heartland of the Middle San Juan

A School for Advanced Research Popular Archaeology Book

Since 2004 the School for Advanced Research (formerly the School of American Research) and SAR Press have published the Popular Archaeology Series. These volumes focus on areas of interest to archaeologists and the broader public. They contain up-to-date archaeological data, described in language that is accessible to a wide audience, and a wealth of images. The resulting volumes reflect SAR's commitment to the dissemination of new ideas and to education at all levels. The complete Popular Archaeology Series can be found at www.sarweb.org.

Also available in the School for Advanced Research Popular Archaeology Series:

First Coastal Californians, edited by Lynn H. Gamble
Medieval Mississippians: The Cahokian World, edited by Timothy R. Pauketat and Susan M. Alt
Living the Ancient Southwest, edited by David Grant Noble
Hisat'sinom: Ancient Peoples in a Land without Water, edited by Christian E. Downum
Mimbres Lives and Landscapes, edited by Margaret C. Nelson and Michelle Hegmon
The Great Basin: People and Place in Ancient Times, edited by Catherine S. Fowler and Don D. Fowler
The Hohokam Millennium, edited by Suzanne K. Fish and Paul R. Fish
The Mesa Verde World: Explorations in Ancestral Pueblo Archaeology, edited by David Grant Noble
The Peopling of Bandelier: New Insights from the Archaeology of the Pajarito Plateau, edited by Robert P. Powers
In Search of Chaco: New Approaches to an Archaeological Enigma, edited by David Grant Noble

For additional titles in the School for Advanced Research Popular Archaeology Series, please visit unmpress.com.

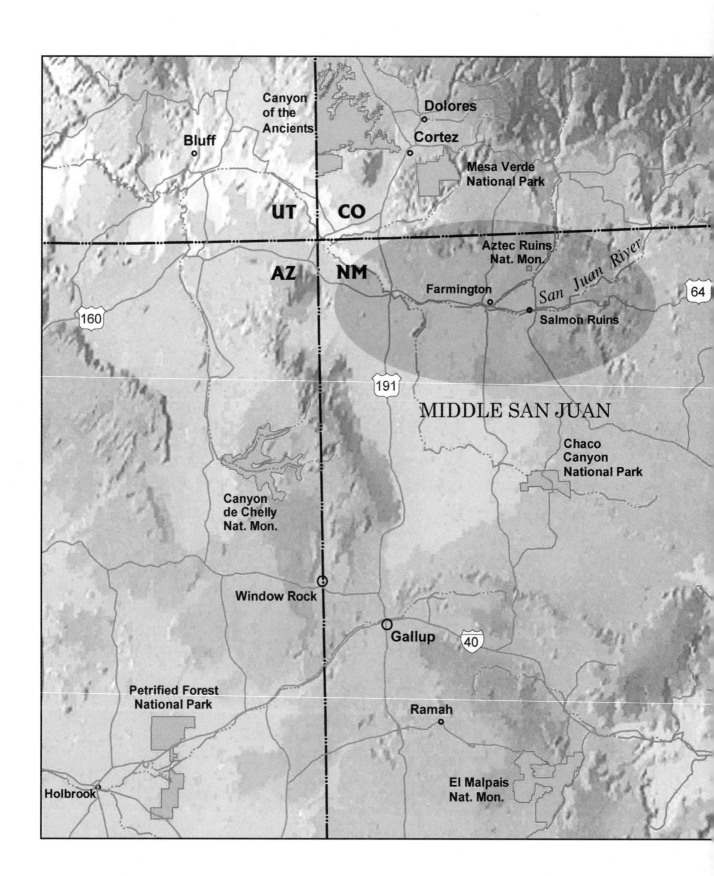

Canyon
of the
Ancients

Bluff

Dolores

Cortez

Mesa Verde
National Park

UT   CO

AZ   NM

Aztec Ruins
Nat. Mon.

San Juan River

Farmington

64

160

Salmon Ruins

191

MIDDLE SAN JUAN

Chaco
Canyon
National Park

Canyon
de Chelly
Nat. Mon.

Window Rock

Gallup   40

Petrified Forest
National Park

Ramah

Holbrook

El Malpais
Nat. Mon.

Aztec, Salmon, and the Puebloan Heartland of the Middle San Juan

Edited by **Paul F. Reed and Gary M. Brown**
Foreword by **David Grant Noble**

SCHOOL FOR ADVANCED RESEARCH PRESS • SANTA FE

UNIVERSITY OF NEW MEXICO PRESS • ALBUQUERQUE

© 2018 by the School for Advanced Research
All rights reserved. Published 2018
Printed in the United States of America

Library of Congress Cataloging-in-Publication Data
Names: Reed, Paul F., editor. | Brown, Gary M., editor.
Title: Aztec, Salmon, and the Puebloan heartland of
the Middle San Juan / edited by Paul F. Reed, Gary M.
Brown; foreword by David Grant Noble.
Description: First edition. | Albuquerque: University of
New Mexico Press: Published in Association with School
for Advanced Research Press, 2018. | Series: School for
Advanced Research Popular Archaeology Series | A
school for advanced research popular archaeology book.
| Includes bibliographical references and index. |
Identifiers: LCCN 2017060735 (print) | LCCN
2018022108 (e-book) | ISBN 9780826359933 (e-book) |
ISBN 9780826359926 (paperback)
Subjects: LCSH: Salmon Site (N.M.)—Congresses.
| Pueblo Indians—New Mexico—Antiquities—
Congresses. | Pueblo Indians—Material culture—New
Mexico—Congresses. | Excavations (Archaeology)—
New Mexico—Congresses. | Pueblo architecture. |
Pueblo Indians—Migrations. | Aztec Ruins National
Monument (N.M.) | San Juan River Valley (Colo.–
Utah)—Antiquities. | BISAC: SOCIAL SCIENCE /
Archaeology.
Classification: LCC E78.N65 (e-book) | LCC E78.N65
A95 2018 (print) | DDC 979.2/59—dc 3
LC record available at https://lccn.loc.gov/2017060735

Cover photograph: courtesy the National Park Service;
photograph by Joel Gamanche
Designed by Lisa C. Tremaine
Composed in Myriad Pro and Arno Pro

Contents

Foreword

David Grant Noble

In the 1970s, when I was first learning about Chaco Canyon, Aztec Ruins, and Mesa Verde, I was informed that Aztec was one of numerous outlying great houses of Chaco Canyon. "Chacoans" built it, lived in it, and eventually left. After their departure, winds then blew in sand and dust that covered roofs and floors. Later, people from Mesa Verde reoccupied and remodeled the building; thus, Aztec West experienced two separate occupations by two distinct cultural groups. As to local Middle San Juan people, they were barely mentioned.

After Earl Morris excavated at Aztec (1916–1921), the Middle San Juan region commonly was considered in its relation to the architecturally stunning centers of Chaco Canyon and Mesa Verde, located to the south and north, respectively. Research in recent decades, however, has stimulated fresh thinking about human history and interactions along the Middle San Juan. In the process, the traditional narrative has shifted.

The authors of *Aztec, Salmon, and the Puebloan Heartland of the Middle San Juan* assert that this region—known as the Totah by Navajos—was, between circa 1000 and 1300 CE, an important and influential cultural and political center in its own right. Given the presence of fertile land, abundant water, and good hunting and foraging, no one should be surprised that people were drawn here in large numbers, thrived, and acquired power, status, and some wealth. To recognize the importance of communities in the Middle San Juan in no way diminishes the significance of Mesa Verde and Chaco; it simply gives credit to many people who have long existed in the archaeological shadow of their famous neighbors.

Popular literature and even sometimes academic texts often give nonspecialists the impression that in ancient times the Southwest was divided into distinct and separate cultural groups. In the Four Corners region, for example, were the Chacoans, Mesa Verdeans, and Kayentans; maps often show what look like territorial borders between them. Paul Reed, Gary Brown, and the scholars who have contributed chapters to this book help to dispel this somewhat distorted concept.

We know from so many examples around the world, past and present, how much peoples of different ethnic and cultural backgrounds interact, even when they are separated geographically and speak different languages. Families relocate, large groups migrate, armed forces go to war and take captives. People travel, visit neighbors, trade, and intermarry. They also exchange thoughts and beliefs and share their cultures. Inevitably, change occurs. The communities of the Middle San Juan were no exception to this pattern; indeed, they were perfectly situated to enjoy and benefit from social, economic, and cultural interactions with their neighbors.

This book is the latest volume in the Popular Archaeology Series, which was born in the 1980s as the School of American Research's annual bulletin, known as *Exploration*. Those magazines developed into books such as *New Light on Chaco Canyon* and *The Hohokam: Ancient People of the Desert*. Later, the series evolved into longer and more comprehensive volumes that include the perspectives of Native American scholars and storytellers.

Our common purpose throughout has been to bring current findings, insights, and knowledge in Southwestern anthropology to a wide general readership. In recent decades, the public has shown a growing interest in, even fascination with, the American Southwest and the history and culture of its Native peoples. The following pages help satisfy a general thirst for knowledge and understanding. It should be noted, too, that archaeologists need the public to know about and appreciate what they do, for as taxpayers, donors, and sometimes grant-application reviewers, we play a significant role in supporting their research.

The Popular Archaeology Series, which is now a collaboration between the presses of the School for Advanced Research and the University of New Mexico, is helping to educate us about American archaeology and to understand why the places where our ancestors lived should be cherished and protected. Reed and Brown devoted much time and effort to bringing this book to fruition, and it will be an invaluable resource for scholars, students, and the general public.

Preface

Paul F. Reed and Gary M. Brown

The idea for this book grew out of conversations we had at the 2012 Pecos Conference, held at Pecos National Historical Park in New Mexico. Among those we talked to was David Grant Noble, who has written the foreword to this volume and edited several books in the Popular Archaeology Series. David encouraged us to pursue the project and produce an easily readable archaeological summary of the often-overlooked Middle San Juan area. Despite some of the challenges along the way, we are very glad we took his advice.

The Middle San Juan lies between the ancient Puebloan homelands of Chaco Canyon (to the south) and Mesa Verde (to the north), positioned somewhat closer to the Mesa Verde region. Most people are much more familiar with these places. Yet archaeologists have studied the Middle San Juan and explored its spectacular ruins for more than one hundred years. Earl Morris's excavations at Aztec West from 1916 to 1921 (sponsored by the American Museum of National History) were among the earliest large-scale projects in the Southwest. Other projects were undertaken in the area in succeeding decades, but none was as intensive as his until the San Juan Valley Archaeological Program (the Salmon Project) was initiated by Dr. Cynthia Irwin-Williams in 1969.

Much of the archaeological research and exploration reported in this volume follows in the footsteps of these two pioneering archaeologists—Morris and Irwin-Williams. We believe that this book and the research completed offers homage to their legends. Their extraordinary efforts to describe and explain the sudden appearance of large towns similar to those at Chaco Canyon, yet well outside the Chacoan regional center, established the foundation for generations of scholars to build on and ultimately to reconsider how and why ancient Puebloan civilization developed as it moved from place to place across the Southwest.

We have a list of people to acknowledge. First and foremost, we wish to thank all of the authors who contributed to this book for working hard and responding to an often-demanding schedule. Jane Kepp coached us all during a workshop and encouraged us to think outside the scholarly box in which we were most comfortable. In addition, her editorial assistance helped improve our first drafts. Two anonymous reviewers provided valuable commentary that allowed us to sharpen our focus and clarify important points in the volume. Our publishers at SAR Press went through personnel changes but nevertheless stood by us and the book project. We appreciate the assistance of, first, Lynn Baca (former director of SAR Press) and Lisa Pacheco (former managing editor of SAR Press) and, subsequently, Sarah Soliz (managing and acquisitions editor for SAR Press) and Michael Brown (president of SAR). We feel strongly that SAR Press's commitment to publishing books that speak to a popular audience is particularly valuable.

Lori Stephens Reed (one of our authors) and Cyresa Bloom, both of Aztec Ruins National Monument, helped find various photographs for use in the volume. Larry Baker (executive director of Salmon Ruins Museum, and one of our authors) was most helpful in providing access to Salmon's archive of images for this book. Catherine Gilman, of Desert Archaeology Inc., produced our regional map of the Middle San Juan area. Both of the editors and two additional contributors to this volume, Lori Reed and Laurie Webster, worked together for several years on research that underpins much of what is presented in these chapters. This research was supported by grants from the National Science Foundation. Additional research that contributes to this endeavor was supported by the Western National Parks Association and Archaeology Southwest.

A Chronology of Middle San Juan Regional History

Dates are given as BCE (before the Common Era) and CE (of the Common Era).

11,000–6000 BCE. This period marks the Paleoindian era in the Four Corners area.

6000–500 BCE. Archaic era peoples inhabit and use the landscapes of the Middle San Juan and surrounding areas for their highly mobile hunting-and-gathering lifestyles. Families begin to supplement their diet of wild resources by planting corn before 1000 BCE.

500 BCE. Basketmaker era peoples first use the Middle San Juan region, practice corn horticulture, and continue to supplement their diets with hunting and gathering.

500–750 CE. The Basketmaker III period marks the occupation of sophisticated subterranean structures known as pit houses. The widespread use of pottery accompanies baskets, and the bow and arrow replaces the atlatl (spear thrower) and spear as the main weapon.

500s CE. Pueblo people establish the first sedentary villages in the area.

600s CE. The population in the La Plata Valley expands, and the valley becomes the population center of the Middle San Juan for the next five hundred years.

700–750 CE. Pueblo people construct the first aboveground masonry (pueblo) structures in the Middle San Juan during the Pueblo I period. The use of pit houses continues, and they are frequently associated with small pueblos.

750–900 CE. The Pueblo I period is characterized by elaboration of architecture and further establishment of large villages, in addition to occupations at numerous smaller farmsteads in parts of the Middle San Juan.

850–875 CE. Initial construction, dated by tree rings, begins at Pueblo Bonito in Chaco Canyon. Pueblo Bonito is to become the largest and most impressive great house in Chaco Canyon and the American Southwest.

900–1140 CE. The Pueblo II period throughout the Southwest is characterized by unit pueblos with masonry roomblocks paired with a distinct type of pit structure known as a kiva.

1050–1075 CE. The Great North Road is built, making a formal connection between Chaco Canyon and the Middle San Juan. The attention of many residents of Chaco Canyon begins to shift to the north and elsewhere in the region. Chacoan outliers appear across much of the greater San Juan Basin.

1090–1105 CE. Salmon Pueblo, a three-story, three-hundred-room great house on the San Juan River north of Chaco, is constructed.

1100 CE. The Puebloan society of Chaco Canyon reaches its peak in population, organizational complexity, and geographic extent.

1100–1110 CE. Construction begins at the western great house at Aztec Ruins, a four-hundred-room structure, on the Animas River north of Salmon Pueblo.

1115–1125 CE. Some Chacoans leave Salmon Pueblo and settle at the Aztec community. Construction begins on the eastern great house at Aztec. Salmon Pueblo is remade as a San Juan–style pueblo. By 1125 Aztec West is the largest great house outside of Chaco Canyon, and the Aztec community together with associated structures is the largest site complex in the Middle San Juan.

1125–1150 CE. The ancient Aztec community, with three great houses, a great kiva, several tri-wall structures, and a host of other dwellings, assumes a primary but short-lived role as the Chacoan center in the north.

1128 CE. This year coincides with the last tree-ring date from a Chaco Canyon great house in the twelfth century.

1130 CE. Organizational stresses begin to cause disintegration of Chacoan society. A prolonged drought begins across the ancient Puebloan region, lasting until 1190. Settlement across the region is disrupted, and the Chacoan system begins to collapse.

1140–1290 CE. The Pueblo III period reflects widespread construction of large multistoried pueblos in new styles not in accordance with the Chacoan great-house architectural tradition.

1150 CE. This year marks the effective end of Chacoan society.

1150–1300 CE. Reduced occupation and habitation are evident at Chaco Canyon.

1200s CE. Post-Chacoan societies emerge across the greater San Juan Basin, with descendant links to Chacoan society but with local and largely autonomous social, political, ritual, and economic institutions. Chacoan traditions persist at Aztec, and great-house construction continues with expansion of Aztec East in the mid-1200s.

1275–1300 CE. Most of the greater San Juan Basin is abandoned by Pueblo peoples. Groups relocate to the Rio Grande and its tributaries, the Zuni-Acoma region, the Hopi Mesas, and other areas.

1280s CE. A catastrophic, intentionally set fire sweeps much of Salmon Pueblo, as part of the abandonment of the great house. Fire destroys much of the western great house at Aztec Ruins, leading to its abandonment.

1300s–1800s CE. Pueblo people make inferred, sporadic visits to great houses in Chaco Canyon.

1450–1500 CE. Ancestral Navajo people migrating from the north settle portions of the Middle and Upper San Juan regions.

1540–1800s CE. Spanish explorers and colonists make sporadic, undocumented visits to Chaco Canyon.

1776 CE. Spanish cartographer Bernardo de Miera y Pacheco produces the first known map of the greater San Juan region. The Dominguez-Escalante expedition traverses the Middle San Juan, noting large ruins in the vicinity of Aztec.

1874 CE. Members of the Wheeler Survey visit the Aztec and Salmon great houses. Timothy O'Sullivan takes photographs of the "Pueblo San Juan," the site that would come to be known as Salmon Ruins.

1878 CE. Anthropologist Lewis Henry Morgan visits Aztec Ruins and produces the first map of the western great house.

1896–1900 CE. The Hyde Exploring Expedition conducts excavations at Pueblo Bonito and other sites under the direction of George Pepper and Richard Wetherill.

1906 CE. The Antiquities Act is passed, protecting Chaco and other sites on public lands from unauthorized excavations.

1916–1921 CE. Earl Morris directs major excavations on behalf of the American Museum of Natural History at the West Ruin of Aztec and limited excavations at several other sites in the Animas Valley.

1923 CE. Aztec Ruins is donated to the National Park Service and becomes Aztec Ruins National Monument through presidential proclamation under authority of the Antiquities Act.

1972–1979 CE. Cynthia Irwin-Williams, her colleagues, and a huge team of students and volunteers undertake the large-scale excavation of the ruins of Salmon Pueblo.

The Ancient Pueblo People of the Middle San Juan Region

Paul F. Reed and Gary M. Brown

A traveler leaves Chaco Canyon on an autumn morning. He walks past the large town of Pueblo Alto on a broad, ancient path known today as the Great North Road, heading into the brilliance and warmth of the desert sun (fig. 1.1). Several hours' journey brings him to a series of monumental buildings at a settlement that would later be known as Pierre's Site. He enjoys a quick bite of cornmeal cakes and beans—an ancient tostada— then he resumes his journey to the north, spending the night at a small pueblo "inn" along the road.

Another long day of walking brings the traveler to the end of the road at an outpost that archaeologists know as Twin Angels Pueblo, named after a picturesque natural rock feature located on the opposite side of the canyon (fig. 1.2). This settlement is similar in design to the great houses of Chaco Canyon, although the scale is much smaller than that of Pueblo Bonito—the center of Chacoan life. To reach his destination, our traveler descends into the deep, wide canyon. A large, swift river comes into sight; the traveler breathes a sigh of relief, knowing that he is nearing his destination. After his journey through the high desert, he doesn't mind wading across the river and rinsing the dirt and sweat from his weary body. He needs to freshen up and get ready for human interaction again.

The year is 1100 CE, and our traveler gazes upon a bustling town, known today as Salmon Pueblo, after the family that homesteaded this part of the fertile San Juan

Figure 1.1. A view looking north along the Great North Road from the Chacoan great house at Pueblo Alto. The Great North Road begins at Pueblo Alto and runs approximately thirty-five miles north to the vicinity of Twin Angels Pueblo. Courtesy of Paul Reed, photographer.

Figure 1.2. An aerial view of Twin Angels Pueblo, a small Chacoan great house. The site is in the middle of the photograph, on the edge of a steep cliff that drops into a large rock shelter. The main portion of the Great North Road ends just south of the site. Courtesy of Paul Reed, photographer.

Valley. Although he has walked for two days, the traveler immediately feels comfortable in this new setting. Salmon has been built in the classic Chacoan style, with massive walls and a towering three-story layout that together recall Pueblo Bonito and other monumental buildings at the man's home in Chaco Canyon (fig. 1.3).

A dozen years later, our traveler leaves Salmon Pueblo, heading north toward the next major river that runs through the Animas Valley. After an easy day's walk, he sees the sprawling community where a huge building is rising from the valley bottom. A smaller yet imposing pueblo sits on the mesa above it, with a road like the one

Figure 1.3. Pueblo Bonito, Chaco's greatest great house, from the overlook point. Readers will note Bonito's towering back wall and massive footprint on the south side of Chaco Canyon. It truly is monumental architecture. Courtesy of Paul Reed, photographer.

the traveler is on leading up to it from the valley below. The cluster of large buildings, ceremonial structures, and numerous smaller dwellings will come to be known as Aztec Ruins when Euro-American homesteaders settle the area centuries after the Pueblo people have left. Aztec and Salmon reflect the Chacoan style of architecture and settlement, with huge buildings that rise over large, open gathering places, or plazas, for local residents and their guests. Like Salmon, the plaza is the only point of entry into the main town at Aztec.

The traveler is greeted by a throng of people. He has been here before to celebrate various occasions, including the summer and winter solstices, which he presided over. His brother is married to a woman from Aztec. The largest building is still under construction, but the massive grouping of rooms on the east side borders a large open area, like the plaza at Salmon, where ceremonies and daily discourse bring people together. The building is very similar to Salmon's and to some of the newer great houses at the man's original home in Chaco Canyon.

The people of Aztec stop their building activities to welcome the visitor. They provide him with food and drink. His announcement takes them by surprise: several prestigious families at Salmon may wish to move to Aztec. The workforce at Aztec already includes a diverse population of migrants from Chaco Canyon in addition to natives of the Animas Valley. In good time, the residents of Aztec and Salmon agree that work will begin on another large pueblo to the east. Aztec is already the largest Pueblo community north of Chaco Canyon, and it is about to become even bigger. Sustained work at these pueblos will eventually result in a group of monumental great houses that rival and even surpass the many buildings in "downtown" Chaco.

The traveler in this narrative was born and raised at Chaco Canyon, where centuries of construction resulted in gigantic masonry buildings with multiple stories—a Pueblo center that attracted people from across the large region we know today as the Four Corners (fig. 1.4). Although many people lived in Chaco for generations, some people migrated from far-flung areas, and others made shorter visits to congregate and celebrate occasions such as the changing of seasons and the passing of years. People shared new ideas from throughout the

area and forged social relationships. They traded various items, some from distant places and some from nearby. Chaco must have been special because people brought exotic items with them, but relatively few tangible goods produced at Chaco were taken back to the outlying communities that participated in these congregations. Many archaeologists think that Chacoan religion was the major attraction and that some gatherings involved pilgrimages.

Chaco Canyon is an arid place with no permanent rivers. Well to the north lie the Rocky Mountains, and major rivers flow from snowy peaks into the canyon and mesa country of the San Juan Basin. The largest is the San Juan River, a major tributary of the Colorado River. In this book, we refer to this part of northwestern New Mexico as the Middle San Juan region. The Animas and La Plata Rivers also flow through this area, providing abundant water not found anywhere near Chaco Canyon. The three rivers converge into one at Farmington, New Mexico, the largest city in the area today.

Often lost in the shuffle between the spectacular Pueblo centers at Chaco Canyon and Mesa Verde, the Middle San Juan is one of the most dynamic territories in the ancient Southwest. Pueblo people lived and died in the area for more than one thousand years before Aztec and Salmon rose and transitioned during the closing decades of the 1200s. The earlier time periods are fascinating, as is the later occupation by Navajo people, who arrived after the Ancestral Pueblo inhabitants had left the area. However, we focus this book on the interval from 1050 to 1300. This interval is relatively brief for an area that was occupied for more than ten thousand years, but understanding the events that occurred in the Middle San Juan during what Southwestern archaeologists commonly call the late Pueblo II and Pueblo III periods is a complex and intriguing endeavor.

Archaeologists divide this interval into the Chacoan and post-Chacoan periods because the expanding influence of Chaco Canyon dramatically transformed Ancestral Pueblo occupation of the Four Corners area. In the late 1000s and early 1100s—two centuries after the first great houses were built at Chaco Canyon—similar great houses emerged at Aztec, Salmon, and elsewhere in the Middle San Juan. Aztec and Salmon are the largest and clearest examples of "Chacoan outliers" in the

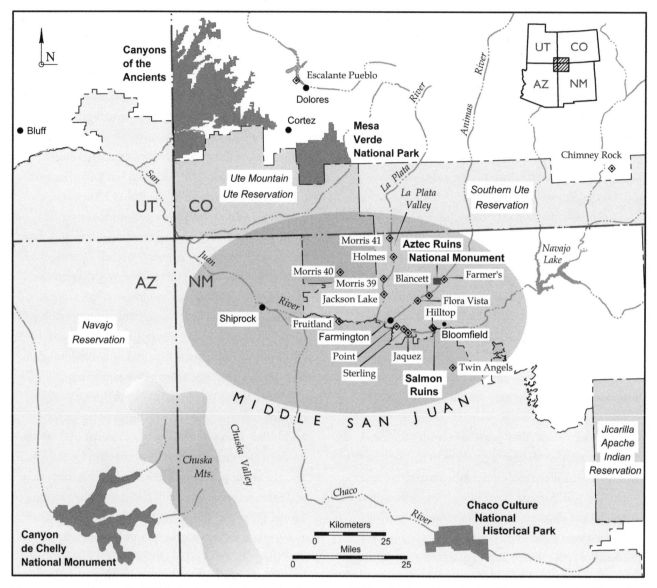

Figure 1.4. A map showing the Middle San Juan region within the Chacoan world. Note the sites of Aztec Ruins, Salmon Ruins, and La Plata Valley. © Archaeology Southwest, 2016.

Middle San Juan, but many pueblos throughout the area also show aspects of Chacoan architecture and other shared characteristics. Other Chacoan outliers are much smaller, however.

The roots of Chacoan society are deep. During the Basketmaker III period, hundreds of years before any great houses were built and half a millennium before Salmon and Aztec dominated the Middle San Juan, large pit-house villages appeared on mesas at the east and west ends of Chaco Canyon. Several hundred people made their homes in Chaco from this time to the next

millennium. During the 800s, construction at the first great houses began in Chaco Canyon. In less than a hundred years, Chaco accelerated into a power drive that produced more than a dozen great houses by the early 1100s. Beyond Chaco, three hundred affiliated sites with Chaco's distinctive architecture were constructed across the modern Four Corners states. At its peak, Chacoan society covered an area larger than the country of Ireland and included tens of thousands of Pueblo people. Chacoan ritual, trade, and social relations dominated the landscape. With no wheeled vehicles, many miles of roadways were constructed along with shrines, trails, and other landscape monuments, which connected the society into a cohesive network.

By 1120, things began to change in Chaco, and things had certainly changed in the Middle San Juan. Construction ceased at great houses in Chaco Canyon while increasing in some other areas, such as Aztec. Many great houses were abandoned or saw reduced population and use. Some archaeologists suggest that severe and sustained drought, which began about 1130, caused the collapse of the Chacoan system. While the drought undoubtedly impacted Chacoan agriculture, the collapse and reorganization of Chacoan society were well under way before the twelfth-century drought. And while Chaco fell into decline, Aztec and other areas rose to prominence. However, the growth of these new population centers began well before the collapse of Chaco.

The authors writing in this book attribute the development of the largest centers at Salmon and Aztec to migration and colonization by people from Chaco Canyon, more than fifty miles south of the Middle San Juan. Although this distance is relatively short, taking only two days on foot, we believe that people with distinct material culture and traditions moved to outlying areas where they can now be distinguished archaeologically from local populations. The impressive scale of construction and numerous unique architectural characteristics are sudden developments at the outliers, unlike at Chaco Canyon, where they evolved over centuries. The great houses at Aztec and Salmon appear to be dominant, but we do not use the term *colony* to suggest that migrants from Chaco exerted coercion or oppression. Chacoan migrants and local leaders worked together while maintaining their identities and connections with their individual homelands. Smaller great houses were built in many communities, some as a result of local emulation of Chacoan building style, and some by smaller groups of Chaco Canyon migrants, perhaps religious leaders and their entourages.

Chaco-style great houses were not the only impressive developments at this time. Sites large and small were built along the San Juan, Animas, and La Plata Rivers. Populations grew as a result of both natural population growth and migration from Chaco and other adjacent

areas into the Middle San Juan. The smaller sites generally lacked Chacoan characteristics, and many were clustered together into villages that had begun to coalesce before the Chacoan period. Chacoan migrations into some of these aggregated communities are evident in the form of exceptionally prominent buildings around which smaller "unit pueblos" are clustered. Some of these prominent buildings are great houses that comprise the nucleus of the village. This distinction between great-house architecture with classic and sometimes subtle Chacoan attributes and the more common, ordinary construction of small pueblos and other houses is one reason that we see Chacoan migrations into existing communities as a key aspect of population growth at this time. At other Middle San Juan sites, direct evidence of Chacoan presence is lacking, and the data support the rise of local leaders who built Chaco-like great houses.

Archaeologists have documented hundreds of Ancestral Pueblo sites in the Middle San Juan during the past century. Prior to this, nineteenth-century settlers described an abundance of ruins that many attributed to the once-powerful Aztecs of Mexico. Local settlers failed to appreciate that Native people were responsible for such monumental construction. However, the Pueblo Indians and their great houses had nothing to do with the Aztecs. The ancient towns in the Middle San Juan were built before the Aztec cities in central Mexico, although Aztec Ruins is stuck with the name, and other references to Mesoamerican people and places remain throughout the Southwest.

Today, those of us engaged in research in the Middle San Juan recognize cultural diversity among the ancient groups that inhabited this area. Even those within a localized area like Chaco Canyon cannot be categorized as one ethnic or tribal group. Skeletal studies have revealed the presence of several distinct biological populations even within Chaco Canyon. These findings indicate that the "Chacoans" were not a homogeneous group of people. On the contrary, at least two or more biological and social groups were present there. The data suggest that Salmon and Aztec were also composed of more than one distinct group: migrants from Chaco Canyon resided with local San Juan groups. When we use the term *Chacoan* in this book, it does not indicate

Figure 1.5. A northward view of tall standing architecture at Salmon Pueblo, 1874, by Timothy O'Sullivan of the Wheeler Survey. Courtesy of the National Archives, Timothy O'Sullivan, photographer.

connection to a single ethnic or biological population. Rather, we use it to refer to specific characteristics, such as architecture, pottery, textiles, baskets, and other material cultural. In addition, we also use *Chacoan* to refer to the larger society of people, to traditions, to social relations, a way of life, and a lasting legacy. Occasionally, we distinguish a combination of traits that is unique enough to suggest that "Chacoan people" can be identified. In these cases, we mean people from Chaco Canyon who had been socialized and trained in fields such as construction and ritual. We try to be clear when we are talking about people or when we are simply referring to artifacts or other materials.

With that in mind, we see the strongest link between Chaco and the Middle San Juan at the great-house communities of Salmon and Aztec (fig. 1.5). At these two places, we do think we can identify Chacoan people and distinguish them from local inhabitants of the San Juan and Animas Valleys. The constellation of Chacoan traits at these two places is remarkably similar to those of Chaco Canyon itself. In these two instances, the data support the hypothesis that large, organized groups of people migrated from Chaco into the Middle San Juan, and we think these migrations were part of a much larger population movement from Chaco into outlying areas to establish colonies at various strategic locations. Although this Chacoan connection is greatest at Salmon and Aztec, the history of Puebloan occupation is longer in many surrounding areas, such as La Plata Valley and areas to the west. We are fascinated, but not surprised, by the appearance of these two important Chacoan outliers in local areas with limited Puebloan presence prior to 1050 (fig. 1.6).

When, how, and why were the towns of Salmon and Aztec established? What roles did they play in the

Paul F. Reed and Gary M. Brown

Figure 1.6. A view from the third story at Aztec West looking over the central kiva within the main roomblock and across the plaza and Chacoan court kiva. Courtesy of the National Park Service, Gary Brown, photographer.

waning years of the Chacoan world? Archaeologists have attempted to answer these questions since the time of archaeologist Earl Morris in the early 1900s. Morris thought that Aztec was a Chacoan colony. More than half a century later, Cynthia Irwin-Williams proposed that Salmon Pueblo also was built by Chacoan colonists. These two pioneering archaeologists theorized that the abandonment of the sites at the end of their Chacoan occupations in the mid-twelfth century was followed by reoccupation by Mesa Verdean peoples in the late twelfth and early thirteenth centuries. Recent work supports the idea that Salmon and Aztec were built by people from Chaco. However, we question the notion of "reoccupation," because both Aztec and Salmon show evidence of continuous habitation and use during the mid-1100s, when abandonment was supposed to have occurred, according to previous scenarios.

While early attempts to answer these questions were based on preliminary data, we now have thousands of tree-ring dates that enable us to pinpoint the time of initial construction at Salmon in the early 1090s and at Aztec in the early 1100s. There is abundant evidence showing the occupation of both sites for almost two hundred years after the initial migration from Chaco. Salmon was the earliest major colony in the Middle San Juan, with Aztec following soon after. Many people migrated directly from Chaco to both Salmon and Aztec, where they joined forces with local people. A substantial group of colonists may have relocated from Salmon to Aztec to help orchestrate the expansion of Aztec after 1120, helping to make it the center of the Middle San Juan. Although several generations of people continued to build and to occupy both communities, we do not think that large migrations from Chaco Canyon took place after this time.

Moving from the "when" to the "how," we can explore the mechanisms by which migrants from Chaco came to the Middle San Juan to help the local people build the great houses of Aztec and Salmon. Our recent research supports the perspectives of Earl Morris and Cynthia Irwin-Williams, who thought that colonization was the key process driving great-house construction at Aztec and Salmon. However, we further suggest that Chacoan migrants collaborated with local populations in this enterprise rather than establishing some kind of military outpost. The locals were active agents in putting the Middle San Juan "on the map" of the Four Corners area. We suspect that Chacoan migration into these agriculturally productive areas helped to provision the population at Chaco Canyon and solidify the network that had been established to obtain imports from outlying areas. At the same time, people in the Middle San Juan, who had already been emulating and interacting with neighbors at the Chacoan great houses, gained prestige and access to exotic items traded through the centralized network (fig. 1.7).

During the Chacoan period, these mixed groups worked together to build the great houses, great kivas, and roads. Extensive trade and interaction resulted in the distribution of unique Chacoan traits across the Middle San Juan. Later, in the post-Chacoan period,

Figure 1.7. A reconstruction of Salmon Pueblo, as it may have appeared in 1100 CE. The figure shows a rainy morning at the pueblo. Note the massive three-story walls, the elevated kiva in the central part of the pueblo, and the great kiva in the plaza. © Salmon Ruins Museum, created by Doug Gann, Archaeology Southwest, Salmon Project, 2006.

various groups built large pueblos that continued to grow over time, a pattern that spread across the Southwest during the next century and even continued after many groups had left the Four Corners area. Although people continued to reside in the great houses during the post-Chacoan period, the Chacoan tradition and style of great-house construction was maintained at few sites in the Middle San Juan. The prime example is Aztec, where people built additions onto the major great houses and reinvigorated many aspects of the Chacoan tradition in an attempt to revive the glory that languished with the demise of Chaco Canyon (fig. 1.8). Most people throughout the Middle San Juan, however, shifted their attention toward new variations of ritual and lifestyle.

Finally, let us consider "why." What factors led some Chacoans to think about migrating to the Middle San Juan? One possible factor was a drought that began in the early 1080s and lasted for almost two decades. This drought was not the first or the greatest to impact farmers at Chaco, but the downturn undoubtedly decreased yields of corn and other agricultural staples.

Construction of great houses at Chaco was at a peak, and the population may have been overloaded by the 1080s, needing additional areas for agricultural production. The fertile, well-watered river valleys of the Middle San Juan were ideal locations to boost agricultural production during a time of drought.

Northward expansion out of Chaco was perhaps under way before the 1080s. Chacoan migrants may have built Chimney Rock Pueblo in the upper San Juan by this time (the site has two tree-ring dates at 1076 and 1093), a site that was used ritually for observing long-term cycles of the moon. Archaeologists have obtained early tree-ring dates from other northern outliers, including the Morris 41 great-house community in La Plata Valley, which has several scattered dates in the late 900s and early 1000s. However, none of the other classic great-house buildings in the Middle San Juan have tree-ring cutting dates or other clear evidence of construction before the 1080s. In contrast, numerous tree-ring dates document construction at Salmon Pueblo around 1090. Salmon represents the first intensive effort by

Paul F. Reed and Gary M. Brown

Chacoans to establish a major settlement in the Middle San Juan.

Chaco Canyon had perhaps reached its carrying capacity in the 1080s; consequently, expansion northward to Salmon was most likely intended to establish a large residential population on the nearest permanent river. Salmon Pueblo was built in an area without other large sites or substantial numbers of people. The landscape was not empty, yet it had sufficient space and arable land for a large group of Chacoan immigrants to partner with local Puebloan groups and to construct a large village on new ground. They built Salmon on the San Juan River to take advantage of this obvious water source. Not much more than a decade after the first large group of migrants settled at Salmon, a second substantial group of Chacoan colonists arrived in the Aztec

community to help organize and build the largest great house ever seen in the Middle San Juan region.

Migration from Chaco Canyon and colonization in the Middle San Juan may have helped to alleviate population pressure at Chaco, but why were the migrants allowed to move into these fertile valleys? The San Juan Valley around Salmon had limited local populations prior to Chacoan migration, but the Animas Valley around Aztec did have a sizable community by the mid-eleventh century. The question is intriguing when considering the occupation of Aztec, which appears to have been emulating Chaco with construction of a relatively small great house in the late eleventh century, probably before construction at Salmon. The likelihood that people in the Middle San Juan were participating in gatherings at the impressive great houses at Chaco Canyon well before

Figure 1.8. This view from outside the western great house at Aztec looks through parallel room suites connected by aligned doorways on the second story. Below the protected roofs, similar room suites on the first story lead toward the plaza, while the exterior wall exhibits the dark banded masonry characteristic of the west facade. Courtesy of the National Park Service, George Schweier, photographer, 2005.

colonization occurred helps us to understand why migrations from Chaco may have been welcome. It also seems likely that participation in religious ceremonies based at Chaco contributed to a social environment in the Middle San Juan that was receptive to colonization.

The tradition of grandiose construction and spectacular ceremonies that attracted throngs of people from far and wide was maintained at the eastern great house at Aztec for a century and a half after our fictional traveler from Chaco brought word from Salmon that they should join forces. However, a long, persistent drought during much of the twelfth century made it difficult. The eastern great house took a long time to complete, but even the last major construction episode entailed massive masonry walls that followed most Chacoan building codes. The occupants of the eastern great house adhered to established Chacoan traditions at the same time that most people in the Middle San Juan lived in locally constructed pueblos that were adopting new non-Chacoan rituals and mechanisms of community organization. By the last century of life in the Middle San Juan—in the 1200s—things were much less standardized and communities appear to have been more internally focused, with much less concern about grand central places like Chaco or Aztec.

Descendants of the traveler in our story continued to live at Aztec and to honor the wonderful legacy that originated at Chaco and continued at Salmon and Aztec. These people constructed additional great-house buildings in the Aztec community as they continued to build and remodel the major great houses. By the year 1200 at Aztec, the community had a pair of gigantic great houses with a massive community structure between them, and a series of other Chacoan-style buildings that included another great house with at least one hundred rooms. Aztec's western great house was deteriorating by this time, and families built ramshackle houses alongside the towering walls and on top of the rubble of collapsed portions of the huge building. Portions of the western great house were used as repositories for deceased relatives, for restricted ceremonies, and as refuse dumps. Similar things were happening at Salmon Pueblo, where small kivas were built inside Chacoan rooms after the Chacoan founders and followers left Salmon and moved to Aztec.

Many local people continued to live at Salmon, but its Chacoan nature was gone. The unifying spirit that gave rise to the Middle San Juan colonies was fading, as was Chaco itself. Some of the newly developing villages in the Middle San Juan probably welcomed those who had lost interest in Chaco and Aztec. Leaders with new ideas and agendas needed people to help them achieve greatness. Puebloan society witnessed considerable fractioning during the long period of drought in the mid-1100s.

The Aztec community and many other sites continued to grow and change in the post-Chacoan period. Many of the authors in this volume tell portions of the Middle San Juan story in this long period (roughly 1140–1290 CE) after Chaco's dominance ended. By the middle 1200s in the region, and across the entire Puebloan landscape, social and economic problems plagued communities as they grew larger and larger. Archaeologists have identified evidence of violent conflict and intervillage warfare during the Chacoan and especially the post-Chacoan period. Some contemporary Pueblo Indians look back at Chaco and its aftermath as a time of excess and strife. Pueblo people adopted new ways of communal life, and their adaptation to changing circumstances prompted migrations to new areas and mingling with new people to once again form mixed communities of locals and newcomers.

With the Chacoan ceremonial and political legacy receding into the past, and with old social institutions stressed to the breaking point, Puebloan families began to leave the Four Corners and many other areas (Chaco Canyon, greater Mesa Verde, Canyon de Chelly, and the greater Kayenta area). With this exodus well under way, a drought from 1272 to 1299 perhaps added the final coup de grâce, as the area evidently was completely depopulated by 1290. Descendants of our traveler migrated from Aztec, Salmon, and pueblos throughout the Middle San Juan to towns toward the east on the Rio Grande and its tributaries; toward the south at Acoma, Zuni, and Laguna; and toward the west and the Hopi Mesas in Arizona.

The authors in this book will continue the narrative we have only begun to sketch here and will fill in some of the details of ancient Puebloan life in the Middle San Juan. Along with H. Wolcott Toll, we explore ancient life at the Pueblo centers of Salmon and Aztec, as well as along the La Plata River. Esteemed scholar Florence Lister recounts a story about Earl Morris and his reconstruction of Aztec's great kiva. Larry Baker reveals the archaeoastronomical significance of certain sites within Salmon and Aztec. Kathy Durand and Ethan Ortega explore everyday life through food, Laurie Webster through clothing, and Lori Stephens Reed through pottery. Mark Varien offers a Mesa Verde archaeologist's take on the Middle San Juan. Finally, Theresa Pasqual of Acoma Pueblo takes us on a deeply felt journey through the ancient Middle San Juan area.

We trust that our readers will enjoy this journey into the ancient Puebloan landscape of the Middle San Juan. This unique region offers compelling stories of interactions with neighboring areas, most importantly Chaco Canyon and Mesa Verde, but also the extensive regions surrounding those prominent places. Chaco, Mesa Verde, and the Middle San Juan regions all played a significant role in the transformation of ancient Puebloan societies into the communities that we know today in parts of northern New Mexico and Arizona. The ancient Puebloan heartland of the Middle San Juan was instrumental in tying together the developments at Chaco and Mesa Verde to create a distinctive blend of old and new, local and nonlocal, produced by people with a long history of migration, interaction, and innovation. The Chacoan colonies in the Middle San Juan created partnerships with local populations, and it was this collaboration that fostered the unique history of the Middle San Juan, which forms one of the pillars of contemporary Puebloan society.

La Plata Layers

2

H. Wolcott Toll

Archaeologists love layers. The layers they talk about the most are layers of soil—stratigraphy—but a place like La Plata Valley has many other types as well. La Plata is one of three permanent streams that converge at the location of modern Farmington, New Mexico, and this convergence provided an extraordinary amount of water for the vast Ancestral Pueblo area. The Navajo word for this remarkable feature is 'Totah,' "where the rivers 'come together.'" The community sites in La Plata Valley centered on great houses located at the mouths of major drainage systems. Though less famous and less well protected than Salmon and Aztec, these settlements were as interesting and distinctive as large sites in the other valleys of the Middle San Juan region.

The combination of historic and modern development and farming, patchy archaeological survey and excavation, and natural processes of erosion makes comparisons among the Pueblo components of the region difficult. Though we know of large buildings in La Plata's drainage, with architecture very similar to that of Chaco Canyon—as well as Aztec and Salmon, two of the largest buildings in the Chacoan world of the late 1000s and early 1100s CE (see chapters 3 and 4)—we do not know of any buildings of similar size. So let us begin with one particular structure and follow its layers out to a broader view of all the natural, cultural, and historical layers of this fascinating area.

Our starting point is the first really complicated structure that my crews from the Office of Archaeological Studies at the Museum of New Mexico dug on our La Plata Highway project, at the site we know as LA 37592. This project was carried out because yet another layer was about to be added to the abundant stratigraphy

of the valley: a revamped highway. All that was present when we began work at the site was a small mound of rocks and dirt that we knew from experience represented a pueblo of several rooms and some surface artifacts. However, the right-of-way fence had protected a very beautiful structure and deposit from the ravages of waterlines and highway construction.

When we realized that a lot was going on under that fence line, we began what would become a relatively lengthy excavation, and I will recount what we found in historical order—early to late—rather than the actual archaeological order in which we see the most recent layers first. The contents of the structure we excavated cover much of the time period central to this volume: the earliest floor was constructed in the 1000s, and the last events occurred there in the early 1200s (fig. 2.1). Although belowground, circular structures are often called kivas, we worry about terms in archaeology, and the term *kiva* brings much baggage that may not be warranted, so I will use the term *pit structure* instead.

In the 1000s the Puebloan world on the Colorado Plateau was already a place of many layers. The builders and occupants—probably the same people—of the structure had a clear idea of acceptable design. As with buildings, designs and materials for artifacts were well known and closely reproduced, a great boon to archaeologists trying to place them in time and space. At the time this structure was built, pottery in La Plata Valley was the familiar black-on-white decorated ware and corrugated grayware. Raw materials for both wares were available locally, and local products made up most of what was in use.

Making a hole big enough for a structure like this one, four meters across and more than two meters deep,

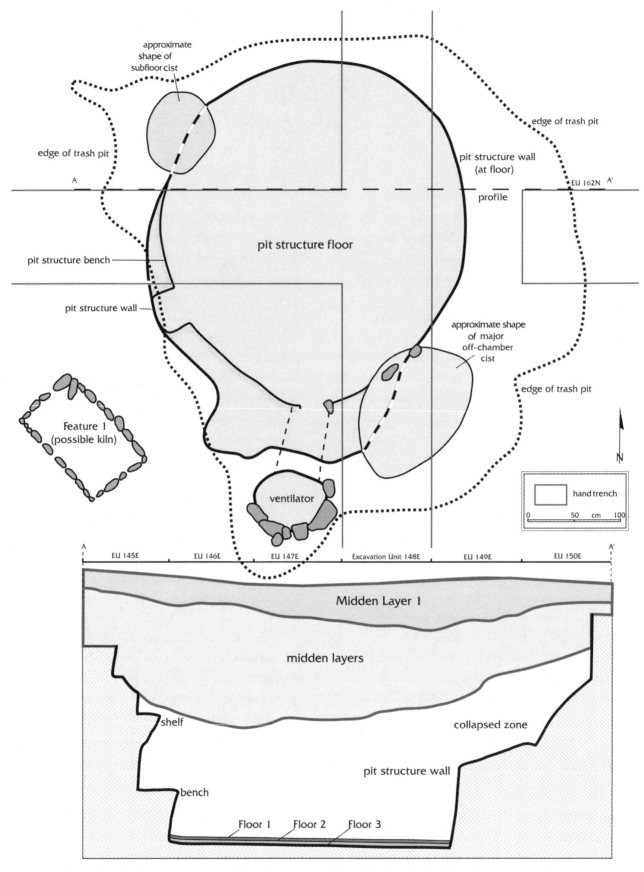

approximate
shape of
subfloor cist

edge of trash pit

edge of trash pit

pit structure wall
(at floor)

EU 162N   A'

A

profile

pit structure floor

pit structure bench

pit structure wall

approximate shape
of major
off-chamber
cist

edge of trash pit

Feature 1
(possible kiln)

ventilator

N

hand trench

0   50   cm   100

A   A'
EU 145E   EU 146E   EU 147E   Excavation Unit 148E   EU 149E   EU 150E

Midden Layer 1

midden layers

shelf

collapsed zone

pit structure wall

bench

Floor 1   Floor 2   Floor 3

Figure 2.1. A plan and profile of a pit structure in La Plata Valley. Courtesy of the Office of Archaeological Studies, Museum of New Mexico.

H. Wolcott Toll

is a lot of work with stone axes and wooden digging sticks. We know that digging disturbed earth here can be difficult, even with modern tools. Once the hole was dug, however, it became an important resource, and its creators made extensive use of it. They built a floor with the required features—a hearth, some storage pits, and a ventilation system including a vertical shaft connected to horizontal tunnel, a deflector to distribute the air flow. Just as the hole was a precious resource, so too was the roof, which was made of logs. La Plata Valley stands out in the ancient Puebloan world as a region rich in natural resources with nearly permanent water, good cropland, favorable growing conditions, and access to a variety of productive ecological zones, but building timbers would have been harder to come by. This fact is demonstrated by how rarely we found good tree-ring samples: we excavated forty-three pit structures spanning around six hundred years and found only two well-represented roofs, the rest having been removed and likely reused prehistorically.

The occupants of the structure remodeled it three times, visible in three overlaid floor surfaces. They maintained the same basic floor and structure design while also making small adjustments: the ventilation system was really quite brilliant but always seemed to need a little tweaking. They used and fixed their floors for perhaps a couple of decades. During this time, potters were making a transition from a painting-and-firing technique in which the paint was all mineral based—ground iron minerals in a vegetal medium—to one in which the paint was all vegetal. This change is a signal time marker for archaeologists.

All pit structures had a finite use life, and after three remodeling episodes this one reached the end of its usefulness, perhaps from erosion of the walls or from vermin or roof problems. The people of the pueblo followed a standard set of procedures when they discontinued their use of a structure. As they left this one, they conducted a formal closing ceremony in which they sacrificed an adult turkey on the hearth and removed the valuable roof timbers for use elsewhere in the area. Archaeologists have been accustomed to describing sites or structures as "abandoned," but we have learned from contemporary Pueblo peoples that that is inappropriate: these places

are still occupied by the ancestors. Moreover, this location continued to be used for many years.

We can see that turkeys were becoming increasingly important to Puebloan life both from the deposition of the turkey at the structure's closing and from the layers of steadily increasing numbers of turkey bones, which represented birds used for food, feathers, and pest control (see chapter 7). Our structure contained a very large storage feature dug through the wall and below the floor, and the last materials put there were hundreds of turkey bones, probably food remains, as well as those used for closing the structure.

With the roof gone, the structure began the process of disintegration common to all buildings without roofs, especially those below ground surface. However, the story of layers was far from over. Initially, we can see the beginnings of the structure's filling and collapse. A layer of clean sand covered the floor and was covered by layers with much more soil and lots of the cobbles that are so abundant on the valley terraces. Cobbles are rocks of varying sizes—larger than pebbles and smaller than boulders—that have been naturally rounded by glacial and riverine tumbling. The number of cobbles in the river valleys is vast, and they were prime building material in spite of their rounded edges, which stack poorly. A majority of sites contain mounds of cobbles and the large amounts of mud mortar required to make them into walls. In valley great houses, people made the added effort to acquire and shape sandstone blocks, with which they made more-permanent and lower-maintenance walls.

As I've said, the soil of the valley is extremely hard, and much of the structure was able to persist with just soil walls that could be plastered. However, some parts of the structure, such as the vent shaft, were constructed of cobbles that were ready to tumble into the open structure. By this time, early Pueblo III, the structure was a bowl-shaped depression in the ground. This time the "hole resource" was used as a place to put household refuse or—an archaeologist's favorite deposit—a midden. We defined five layers in this refuse, which contained thousands of pieces of flaked stone, broken pottery, and animal bones. In the pieces of pottery the shift to organic paint is very clear and, along with the design styles, shows that the transition took place well into the 1100s, approaching the 1200s. And yet even that nice archaeological hallmark indicates complexity in the social layers. For while organic paint became prevalent, mineral paint is still present. Some of that is from the mixture of later deposits with earlier deposits and the introduction of older vessels, but it is also probably found because some potters were still painting their pots in the old way. This finding reminds us that the valley was a large area with a lot of people in it and thus diverse in terms of social norms and traditions.

Within the upper layers of the structure we found more evidence of its importance and persistence, showing how the concept of "abandonment" is inaccurate. Two children were buried in its fill. We have found this method of marking continued connection to place in a number of similar structures throughout the valley.

The final layer in the structure reminds us of another result of many people living in an advantageous but not always easy place. In this layer we found the intentionally disarticulated remains of eight to eleven different people. The people were of different ages, perhaps as might have been found in a family group. We cannot know why they met a grim end, but we know that through time in the valley and in the region they were not the only ones who did. It has been suggested that they became regarded as witches and were thus disposed of; perhaps their deaths resulted from territorial disputes, perhaps ethnic replacement.

The people who chose this location knew it had a deep history and had seen many changes. In the 500s, hundreds of years before our structure was built, the region's people, who were first experimenting with pottery, established a settlement that extended from very near where the structure would be to a wide rincon across the valley. Were these people the ancestors of those who built the structure we excavated? Around 600, dramatic changes in house form and methods of pottery making took place among the residents of this place, big enough changes that we suspect a different group of people moved in, but with enough overlap that there may have been a melding of peoples rather than a complete replacement of one by another. After about a century and a half, even the river was not enough to compensate

for the dry period that descended on the region, and the population moved. They did not leave the valley, but they moved within it to a higher, cooler, and wetter part (in modern geographical terms, Colorado). It was not until the 900s that large numbers of people returned to the lower part of the valley. The several major movements up and down the valley that took place over its fourteen hundred years of occupation had strong climatic drivers and, of course, major social implications that sometimes included violence.

The people of La Plata lived and farmed in the valley over many generations and were clearly well informed about technologies and practices throughout the Chacoan world, including elaborate water collection and distribution systems developed by Chaco Canyon farmers in their harsher environment. The other rivers in the Middle San Juan—the San Juan, close to Salmon, and the Animas, close to Aztec—are far larger and more difficult to control. La Plata River occasionally floods, but it would have been easier to divert onto its expansive floodplains. While La Plata Valley would have been especially well suited to crop irrigation, we have no direct evidence that people were irrigating there. However, the large long-term populations evident in La Plata make a very strong argument that people of the valley had a highly successful farming strategy that probably included irrigation.

From the early 1000s to around 1200, the extended family group living at LA 37592 built a series of rooms to the north and northeast of the pit structure, as well as storage pits and a feature we think—from its size and shape, the layers within it, and others in the region—was a pottery-firing feature or kiln. Through time, people built a number of small pueblos like this one, consisting of some rooms and one or more pit structures. As at this one, parts were lived in at times and reoccupied after intervals. These pueblos would have been within sight of one another, and doubtless the people in them interacted.

Within the La Plata Valley were groups of individual pueblos that we consider to have been communities of people. LA 37592 is within the community we call Jackson Lake. We have identified several communities in the valley (fig. 2.2), and several—perhaps four—included

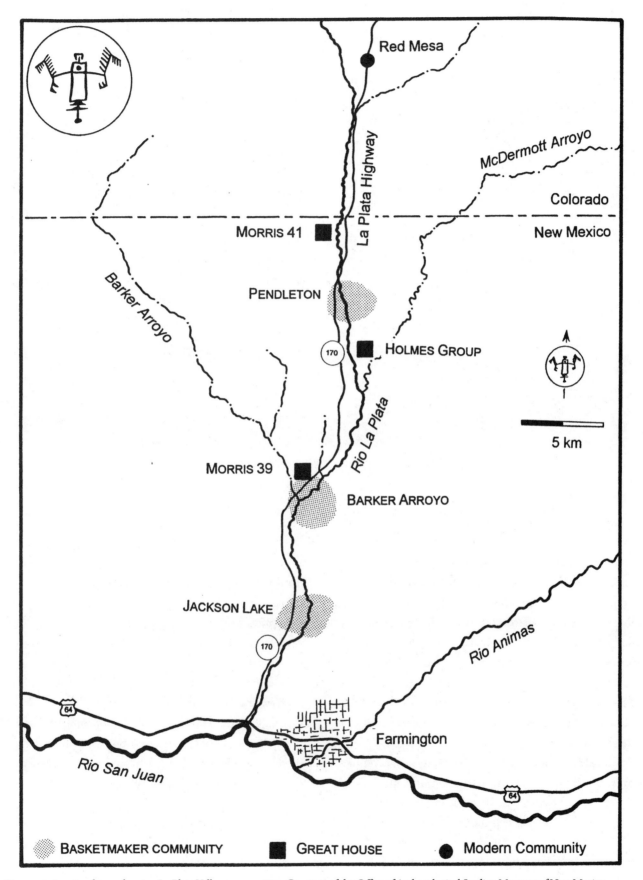

Red Mesa

McDermott Arroyo

La Plata Highway

Colorado

New Mexico

MORRIS 41

PENDLETON

Barker Arroyo

170

HOLMES GROUP

Rio La Plata

5 km

MORRIS 39

BARKER ARROYO

JACKSON LAKE

170

Rio Animas

64

Farmington

Rio San Juan

64

BASKETMAKER COMMUNITY   GREAT HOUSE   Modern Community

Figure 2.2. A regional map showing La Plata Valley communities. Courtesy of the Office of Archaeological Studies, Museum of New Mexico.

Figure 2.3. A kiva depression overlooking La Plata Valley. Courtesy of H. Wolcott Toll, photographer.

structures different from the others: more massive, more carefully built, with specialized areas that would have accommodated larger numbers of people, a means for residents of the community to participate in community functions. These communities include great-house sites that functioned similarly to the way Salmon and Aztec did, although they were of smaller size than Salmon and Aztec. We are not sure if the large structure east of LA 37592 was a great house for the Jackson Lake community, but we do know of the remains of a probable great kiva in a commanding location overlooking the site and its neighbors (fig. 2.3).

The interaction of diverse and widespread communities was the essence of the Chacoan world, of which the communities in the La Plata Valley were clearly a part. Chaco Canyon is well known for having very high levels of imported materials of many kinds: pottery, turquoise, large building elements, and exotic items such as copper and even macaws and cacao. The people of La

Plata clearly participated in these exchange networks as well but apparently to a lesser degree. They had pottery from other regions, such as western New Mexico and northeastern Arizona, and nonlocal materials, such as obsidian and turquoise, but in much smaller relative quantities than sites of all types in Chaco had.

Great houses in Chaco are known for their exotic goods, and although basic household furnishings were similar in Chaco and La Plata Valley, Chaco is notable for how few axes have been found there, whereas they were abundant in the valley. No doubt some of these tools were used for the task we now associate with them—cutting trees—but experiments have shown that they were probably more useful for field clearing and tilling.

To a considerable degree, people in La Plata were in a better place to be largely self-sufficient. For example, around half of the utility pottery dating to the 1000s in Chaco came from a source to the west, the Chuska

Figure 2.4. The great house at Morris Site 39 in La Plata Valley. Courtesy of Carnegie Institution for Science, Washington, DC.

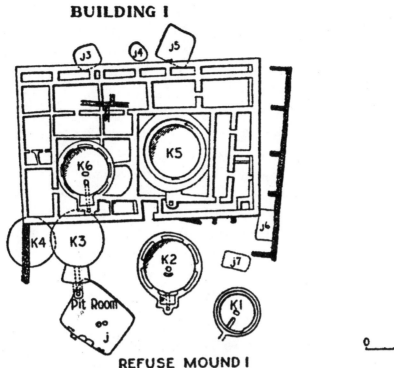

BUILDING I

REFUSE MOUND I

PRINCIPAL PORTION, SITE 39

Mountains and Valley. That source is close to the same distance from Chaco as it is from the mid–La Plata Valley, but that pottery, while present in La Plata, makes up only a very small percentage of the pottery found there. I think this difference was the result of people in Chaco and the Chuska Valley having residences in both places. Unlike Chaco, the people of La Plata also had access to the full suite of materials needed for pottery production: fuel, clay, and water. Part of the discrepancy may be attributable to the natures of the archaeological samples of Chaco and La Plata, but it cannot account for the magnitude of the difference. Whereas more great-house structures have been excavated in Chaco than in La Plata, many smaller habitation sites have been excavated in both places, and the differences remain.

It is more difficult to identify exports than imports into a region in categories other than ceramics and stone. Ceramics with tempers like those in the Middle San Juan occur in other areas, including Chaco, but not in

quantities like those from the Chuska Valley. Since we know that local communities were participating in the greater Chacoan world, what could they have contributed? The great agricultural potential of La Plata Valley relative to many other areas strongly suggests that food would have been a viable candidate (see chapter 3). Food is far harder to source than pottery, but early results from new techniques show that corn was transported to places distant from where it was grown.

One important question that awaits more knowledge of La Plata great houses—indeed, all great houses—is how great houses on local and regional scales related to one another. Especially in the late 1000s and early 1100s, the great houses in La Plata Valley conform to contemporary building styles in many parts of the Chaco sphere (fig. 2.4), which extended from south of Chaco to the Middle San Juan to Mesa Verde to southeastern Utah to northeastern Arizona. People from other communities within the valley and beyond must have come to these major villages for events of varying scales scheduled by leaders knowledgeable about ritual and seasonal cycles.

The Holmes Group, located midway up the valley, was a settlement at least a kilometer long from north to south and included great kivas, great-house roomblocks, and landscape features called "roads." Roads symbolized connections among sites; they preserve poorly, but their presence leaves little doubt that they connected major La Plata sites to the other communities of the time. As at Aztec, an easy (in those days) distance to the east, use of the sites extended to around 1300. Although not recognized by the National Park Service or other entities, La Plata great-house communities were major components of the social,

economic, and religious environments of the tenth through fourteenth centuries.

While it is possible and very interesting to take the layers even further, I will stop my discussion at the Chaco. I have no doubt that all of these layers—the LA 37592 pit structure, the pueblo of which it was part, the Jackson Lake Community, La Plata Valley—contributed to the Chacoan layer. Their influence is visible in the changes in architecture and ceramics, in the specialized features of the community sites and great houses, and in the landscape features that were built to connect the many widespread parts of the Chacoan and Puebloan worlds. For centuries, the valley was a place of remarkable populations, and we see evidence of their achievements in the layers they left behind.

Ancient Lifeways at Salmon Pueblo on the San Juan River

Paul F. Reed

The plaza at Salmon Pueblo bubbles with life. Babies cry, children play, dogs bark, turkeys gobble. Men chip arrowheads and plan hunting trips. Women laugh as they work together, some grinding corn, some sewing clothes or stitching sandals, others rolling clay into coils for pottery.

The year is 1100 CE. Across the Atlantic Ocean, Europe is convulsed by wars as medieval kings clash on faraway battlefields. Castles dominate the skyline. Not far from Salmon Pueblo, structures similar to European castles have appeared at Chaco Canyon—huge masonry buildings we now call great houses. From Chaco these monumental buildings have spread across the greater San Juan country, too. Like European castles, their main purpose is to project social power visibly across the Puebloan landscape (fig. 3.1).

In the late eleventh century, the vanguard of Chacoan immigrants arrived on the San Juan River and began to cut wood, gather stone, and identify the best clay and mortar sources in order to build one of the first

Figure 3.1. A three-dimensional reconstruction of Salmon Pueblo as it may have appeared in 1100 CE. The image shows the massive footprint of Salmon Pueblo on the first terrace above the San Juan River floodplain (to the right and background in the illustration). © Salmon Ruins Museum, created by Doug Gann, Archaeology Southwest, Salmon Project, 2006.

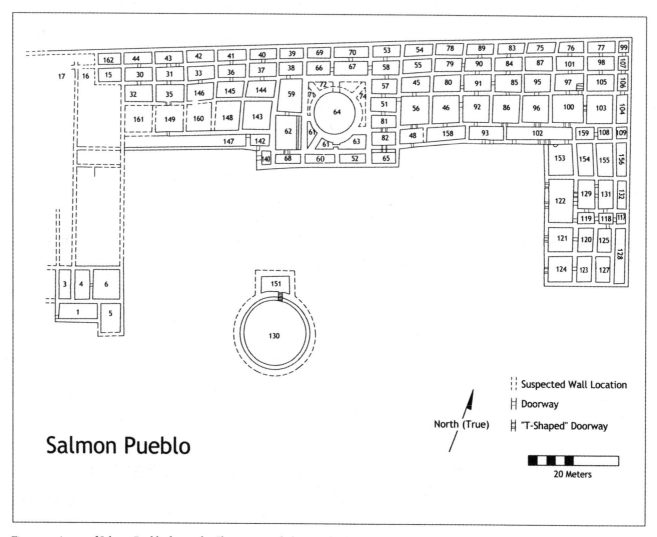

Figure 3.2. A map of Salmon Pueblo during the Chacoan period, showing the distribution of residential room suites and overall pueblo layout. © Salmon Ruins Museum.

and largest great houses outside Chaco Canyon. As built on the north bank of the river, Salmon Pueblo was a three-hundred-room great house, with three stories and a great kiva in its plaza. Its form was classically Chacoan: an E-shaped building facing south and containing a second-story elevated kiva in a direct line north of the great kiva (fig. 3.2). The site was massive, covering more than two acres and towering perhaps thirty feet along its north-facing back wall.

Although its resident population ebbed and flowed, Salmon Pueblo was home to several hundred people for most of the time between 1090 and 1285. Salmon built up to a population of probably two hundred people by 1120, at the peak of the Chacoan era. In the subsequent

early San Juan period, the population declined as many of the original Chacoan immigrants left; perhaps as few as one hundred people lived at Salmon by 1175. In the succeeding late San Juan period, however, the population rebounded and, indeed, reached its peak for the entire two-hundred-year period. By 1260, perhaps four hundred people made Salmon Pueblo their home.

The name of Salmon Pueblo derives not from a fish but from a family, led by Peter Salmon of Indiana, who homesteaded the area beginning in 1877. We don't know what the native Puebloan inhabitants called their dwelling. We do know that they built their pueblo on the north bank of the San Juan River using thousands of wooden beams, cut between 1086 and 1090, and several million carefully shaped sandstone slabs. The builders of this wondrous dwelling—ancient Puebloan architects, planners, and masons—migrated from Chaco Canyon to the Middle San Juan region in the late eleventh century and recruited local Puebloans to join them in their efforts.

The founding of Salmon Pueblo around 1090 was a watershed in the history of the Middle San Juan. It represented the first commitment by a large number of Chacoan colonists to settle a new area outside Chaco Canyon. The shift northward from Chaco Canyon has been attributed to various factors, including changing climatic conditions in the late 1000s. Although Chaco continued as one of the primary centers of ancient Puebloan life into the early 1100s and beyond, the communities built in the Middle San Juan, such as Aztec and Salmon, as well as those built farther north in the greater Mesa Verde region, indicate a change in the focus of activities and a broader geographic spread of Chacoan and post-Chacoan culture by the early 1100s.

Daily life at Salmon Pueblo focused on a few important, universal concepts—food, water, shelter, and social interaction—and the pueblo's residents depended primarily on a trio of domesticated crops for their diet: corn, beans, and squash. These plants were grown in fields adjacent to Salmon, along the floodplain of the San Juan River; on terraces above the river and next to tributary streams; and probably in dry upland locations dependent on rainfall. In addition to these domesticated crops, the Salmonites made use of a broad variety of natural plants for food, including tansy mustard, goosefoot, spurge, purslane, pigweed seeds and greens, yucca fruits, prickly-pear pads, piñon nuts, juniper berries, chokecherry berries, and wild onions. Plants used as medicines or in ceremonial matters often overlapped with those used for food. Corn pollen, for example, is used ritually and sometimes medicinally by the modern Pueblo people and was probably used by the residents of Salmon and other great houses. Spruce and ponderosa tree bark, along with juniper boughs, were used ceremonially or medicinally at Salmon. Ephedra, commonly known as Mormon tea, was probably brewed as a hot beverage and perhaps used as a cure for intestinal and other disorders.

The women of Salmon used handstones called manos to grind corn into meal on large slabs, or metates.

They then shaped the meal into flat cakes, similar to what we call tortillas today, and cooked them on flat stones, or comals, on or near hearths. The Chacoans at Salmon also grew a different type of corn than later occupants did. Chacoan corn was mostly of flint or popcorn varieties, which were larger, were more uniform, and produced more kernels per cob than the flour varieties favored by the post-Chacoan inhabitants of the San Juan. Furthermore, Chacoan grinding facilities held more of the basal grinding slabs known as metates and were able to produce more cornmeal. These findings suggest that Chacoans took a more intensive and organized approach to corn production (fig. 3.3).

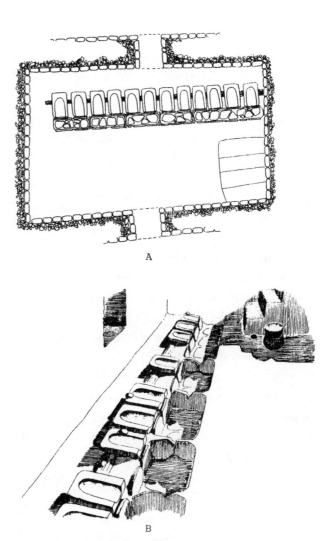

A

B

Figure 3.3. An artist's reconstruction of a row of grinding stations in Chacoan Room 97W. This room contained an astounding twelve metates that allowed for the production of large quantities of ground cornmeal. © Salmon Ruins Museum.

The only domestic animals in the Puebloan world were dogs and turkeys. Turkeys were domesticated as early as 600 CE and were important sources of feathers, bones, and meat (see chapter 7). Particularly during the later occupation at Salmon, after 1150, turkeys were kept in pens and eaten frequently. Dogs are ubiquitous in most human settlements, past and present. Pueblo villages were no exception, and Salmon had its share of them. Dogs were used to help with hunting and carrying loads and as general companions. Dogs in Native America were generally used for food only as a last resort in times of starvation, and we have no evidence of such use at Salmon. Archaeologists have recovered canine bones from Salmon, and it seems clear that dogs were important companions as well as sources of labor for the people.

In the making of jewelry and other ornaments, Salmon artisans reached the peak of their skills. They worked several species of marine shell; minerals such as hematite, jet, and turquoise; and even common materials like bone and siltstone. These artisans painstakingly carved beads from the shells, stones, and bones and then strung them together into amazing necklaces and bracelets. Some of these items were purely for personal adornment, while others were used in rituals and ceremonies.

Several objects of inferred ceremonial importance were found during the excavation and study of Salmon Pueblo. Most significant, perhaps, was a carved green sandstone lizard effigy found near the floor of the Tower Kiva. Research into Puebloan ethnography suggested that the effigy represented Lizard Woman, an important mythological figure (fig. 3.4). Other ceremonial items found at Salmon include two frogs (in the form of tadpoles) carved out of turquoise, a bird effigy made of hematite (a red mineral), and several bird and animal effigies made of fired pottery (fig. 3.5). Very similar frogs have been found at Pueblo Bonito and Aztec, and one researcher suggested that the frogs may have been made by a single craftsman, given the high degree of similarity in their form and manufacturing technique.

Salmon Pueblo was planned and constructed in a deliberate fashion, and it is clear that leaders, perhaps religious leaders, were responsible for organizing the effort. Excavations at Salmon revealed one burial from

Figure 3.4. A lizard effigy from the floor of Tower Kiva at Salmon Pueblo. This artifact is believed to have had ceremonial importance for the pueblo's inhabitants. © Salmon Ruins Museum.

the Chacoan occupation that represents an unusual individual. This elderly man was buried with a bow; nine cane arrows that were probably ceremonial; four bone awls that were originally in a bag; a wooden paho (prayer-feather holder); a robe of fur or feather cloth; four ceramic bowls, all of San Juan manufacture but each San Juan bowl had a distinct design; and a wrapping of finely woven mats (see chapter 8). Salmon's principal archaeologist, Cynthia Irwin-Williams (see sidebar), suggested in the 1970s that this man was a leader in a bow or other ceremonial society at the pueblo. With the special treatment this individual received upon his death, it is clear that he was an important man.

Salmon and Aztec were built in fertile alluvial valleys next to some of the largest rivers in the northern

Figure 3.5. These two ceremonial frog effigies (in tadpole form) were found in Room 100 at Salmon Pueblo. Room 100W also contained two turkey burials and two macaw burials. The room clearly had ceremonial importance at the pueblo. © Salmon Ruins Museum.

Southwest. With the development of water-management techniques in Chaco during the 1000s, it is not surprising that Chacoans moved northward to areas where these newly developed technologies could be implemented on a larger scale. The area around Aztec contains evidence of at least two ancient irrigation ditches, first documented by John Newberry during an 1859 expedition. Archaeologist Earl Morris identified several ditches along the Animas River between Farmington and Aztec that provide further evidence of the Puebloans' skill in managing and moving water. The available evidence indicates that both Salmon and Aztec produced large quantities of corn, and in the case of Salmon, some of this corn may have been exported as ground meal.

One challenge faced by Salmon's residents throughout its history was the flooding of the San Juan River. Evidence of ancient flooding was found during excavations at Salmon, including flood deposits in rooms on both the southwest and southeast corners and in the great kiva. The latter structure was reroofed and perhaps entirely rebuilt in the mid-1260s, and its final form included a high (perhaps two-meter) cobble-and-dirt berm that encircled the kiva and functioned as a flood-control facility.

It is my view that the power of the San Juan River was greater than the Chacoans had anticipated. About two hundred meters away from the river, Salmon was built too close to the water during a period of drought in the late 1080s and early 1090s, when the flow was lower than average. When the river returned to full discharge, the Chacoans at Salmon realized their mistake. In

comparison, Aztec West—initiated around 1105 and complete by 1120—was built more than four hundred meters from the Animas River, a stream with a discharge and flow no more than half that of the San Juan. The Chacoans at Salmon, realizing that the location of the pueblo would not meet their needs, apparently moved to Aztec and helped to build Aztec East, the symmetrical partner of Aztec West, whose construction began in the 1120s. At Aztec, a different group of Chacoan migrants, with close ties to Pueblo Bonito, had much more success, as Gary Brown discusses in chapter 4.

The mid- to late 1100s, after the Chacoans had left, were a relatively quiet time at Salmon. Only part of the original founding group of local Pueblo people then lived at the site. With Chacoan leadership gone, these residents were free to modify the pueblo according to their own needs. Thus, we see the conversion of Salmon's large square living rooms to kivas; room 96W was apparently the first to be converted in the 1120s. Other rooms followed. By the mid-1200s, the locals had built more than twenty kivas into the rooms at Salmon and placed more in the plaza at several points (fig. 3.6). Their need for so many kivas highlights social and ceremonial differences between these local San Juan groups and the earlier Chacoan residents, who provided continuity at Salmon through the 1100s.

The twelfth-century residents of Salmon were subsequently joined by other people from the surrounding Middle San Juan region. We can trace developments similar to those in the north, in the Mesa Verde region, from about 1190 to the 1280s. Larger and larger sites were

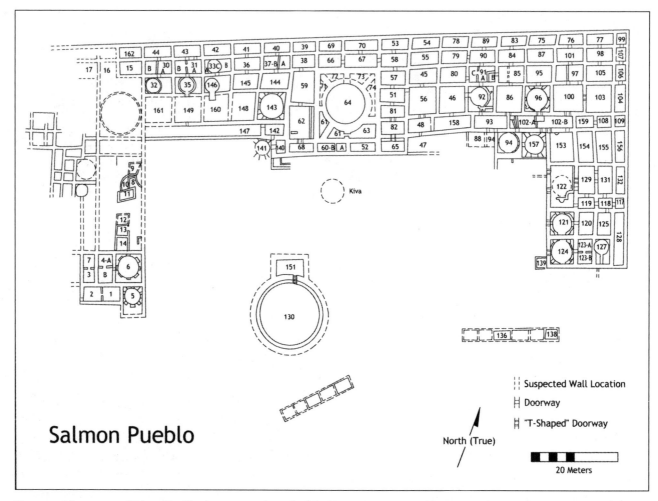

Figure 3.6. A layout map of Salmon Pueblo, about 1250, at the peak of the San Juan occupation of the site. Note the many kivas that were present by this time in the pueblo building. © Salmon Ruins Museum.

built across the greater San Juan region. The numbers of people living in individual pueblos and across the region reached a maximum. And in the absence of the Chacoan socioeconomic and religious system, local leaders were free to make their own decisions.

In contrast to the original interpretation of the 1200s at Salmon, we no longer view migration from the greater Mesa Verde region to the north as the primary cultural influence. Certainly people migrated to and from many areas of the ancient Puebloan Southwest in the 1200s (and in other times). However, architectural and ceramic evidence from Salmon does not indicate a large migration of people from the north (see chapter 10).

In late 1270, tragedy struck Salmon, and it was completely abandoned by 1290. More than twenty children

and several adults died in a short span of time and were cremated atop Salmon's Tower Kiva. At the same time, most of the remaining rooms and kivas at the site were intentionally fired. In fact, several rooms that held stored corn burned so hot the walls were oxidized to a bright orange.

We're not sure how these Salmon residents died; epidemic disease is certainly a strong possibility. While we cannot rule out the possibility of warfare, Salmon lacks the strong indications of warfare that numerous sites across the Four Corners area exhibit. It is possible that conflict with either neighboring Puebloans or an outside group brought trouble to Salmon. In any case, the loss of so many young people was devastating for Salmon's inhabitants, and they left the Middle San

Paul F. Reed

Juan region in short order. The living history of Salmon Pueblo came to an abrupt halt.

The amount of corn charred by fire in several rooms leaves little doubt that the people were not destitute nor on the verge of starving. Aztec has similar rooms in which large quantities of corn were burned as the pueblo was abandoned. These findings seriously challenge the long-held notion that the Pueblo people of the Four Corners were starving in the late 1200s, ultimately forced out of their ancestral homes and homeland by drought. To be clear, there was a drought—the so-called great drought—from roughly 1272 to 1299, which clearly had effects on Puebloan agricultural and other food-producing activities. But the huge volume of burned corn at Salmon and Aztec is clear proof that corn was abundant when the sites and the entire region were abandoned.

Seasonal remains from the harvest in various rooms and kivas at Salmon Pueblo signal that people departed in the autumn of that fateful year. As people left, they had plenty of corn to eat on the journey and probably sufficient corn to plant the following spring.

Abandoned, largely burned, and slowly crumbling under the ravages of time and nature, Salmon Pueblo was absent from the archaeological and historical record until 1874. Visits by itinerant Native Americans and Spanish travelers undoubtedly occurred during this six-hundred-year interval, but we have no record of any of these visits. In October of 1874, photographer Timothy O'Sullivan of the Wheeler Survey visited Salmon. O'Sullivan identified the site as a "characteristic ruin of the Pueblo San Juan" and made a number of wet-plate photographs of the site from various angles (fig. 3.7). The earliest twentieth-century photographs of the site are from the mid-1960s, and none of the standing architecture visible in O'Sullivan's photographs is present. Clearly, the highest portions of the pueblo collapsed or were knocked down in the intervening ninety years (fig. 3.8).

Salmon reemerged into the historical record in the late 1960s. The land containing the ancient pueblo was put up for sale, and it was purchased by the San Juan County Museum Association. The association subsequently sold the land to San Juan County and entered into a lease

Figure 3.7. One of Timothy O'Sullivan's photos of Salmon Pueblo in ruins, 1874, during the Wheeler Survey. This exposure was taken from a point northwest of the pueblo, looking southeast. The view is of the long back, north wall of Salmon Pueblo. Readers will note the central mound in the wall, which marks the location of the filled-in Tower Kiva; also note the high sections of remnant third-story architecture visible at several points along the wall. Courtesy of the National Archives, Timothy O'Sullivan, photographer.

Figure 3.8. Another of Timothy O'Sullivan's photographs of Salmon Pueblo in ruins, 1874, during the Wheeler Survey. This photograph was taken from a point within the pueblo, along the western roomblock (not visible in photo). The view is to the north, again showing remnant third-story architecture, along with one of O'Sullivan's helpers in the middle of the frame and a second wet-plate camera on the right edge of the image. Courtesy of the National Archives, Timothy O'Sullivan, photographer.

agreement to manage the property. High on the list of priorities for Salmon was recruitment of a renowned archaeologist to direct excavations at the site. Cynthia Irwin-Williams was this person. She began work at Salmon in 1970 and developed the San Juan Valley Archaeological Program (the Salmon Project) to understand Chacoan society in the northern Southwest. Excavations, analysis, preservation and stabilization, and writing on the Salmon Project continued until 1980. Finally, through the efforts of Archaeology Southwest and a hybrid team of old and new Salmon researchers, a comprehensive final report was finished on the project in 2006.

The uniqueness of Salmon Pueblo began with the cross-cultural diversity of its founding members: architects , builders, and families from Chaco Canyon, and individuals and families from the San Juan River area. This combination produced the amazing site that survives to this day, more than nine hundred years after its construction. The history of Salmon over its two hundred years of existence is a deep-rooted narrative of ancient Puebloan life in the Middle San Juan. We continue today to seek new methods and data in our quest to understand the details of life at Salmon Pueblo and the richness it has brought to modern Pueblo people.

Paul F. Reed

CYNTHIA IRWIN-WILLIAMS

Any telling of the story of Salmon Pueblo would not be complete without a discussion of Cynthia Irwin-Williams's (1936–1990) pivotal role. She was recruited by Alton James and the San Juan County Museum Association to initiate excavations at Salmon Ruins in 1969. Irwin-Williams had primarily studied earlier hunter-gatherer groups (Paleoindian and Archaic) before taking on the Chacoan site at Salmon. But she quickly adapted to working with the complexities of a massive Chacoan great house and assembled a crackerjack team of archaeologists, staff, and students. From 1970 to 1979, her teams excavated Salmon Ruins, conducted multiple analyses, and began to unravel its mysteries (fig. 3.9).

Irwin-Williams's personal story is remarkable. She became interested in archaeology early in life and was mentored by Marie Wormington (through the Colorado Archaeology Society) as a high school student. After completing her bachelor's degree at Radcliffe, she was one of the first women enrolled in graduate school at Harvard University, where she suffered the indignity of listening to class lectures from the hallway because her presence inside the class was barred by diehard defenders of male privilege. Persevering, she was one of the first women awarded a doctorate from Harvard in 1963.

Hired by Eastern New Mexico University at Portales, Irwin-Williams quickly became known as a rainmaker in Southwestern archaeology. She excelled at working with people and tapped into multiple sources of funding for her archaeological research. Her fund-raising efforts on the Salmon Project eventually exceeded $5 million and made the decade-long research project a success. The Salmon excavations, however, were much more than just a scientific enterprise. Irwin-Williams found it very fulfilling to work with enthusiastic local residents to develop the site and help build the San Juan County Archaeological Research Center and Library and Salmon Ruins Museum facilities, which ensured that the Salmon work would provide a foundation for many years of public education and research (fig. 3.10).

"Throughout her career Cynthia displayed an energy and dedication to archaeology that few can equal," observed archaeologist and original Salmon Project member Lynn Teague. "She was also a loyal friend, extraordinarily generous in some cases, to people that she met as colleagues and as students" (fig. 3.11).

Figure 3.9. Cynthia Irwin-Williams inside a room at Salmon Ruins, 1973. A life-long Francophile, Dr. Irwin-Williams is wearing her signature beret in this photo as she examines the Chacoan masonry veneer (facing) patterns in the room. © Salmon Ruins Museum.

Figure 3.10. Cynthia Irwin-Williams in the camp at Salmon Ruins, 1974. Dr. Irwin-Williams was proud of her skill with a shovel or trowel and frequently "moved dirt" right alongside her students and staff. © Salmon Ruins Museum.

Figure 3.11. A portrait of Dr. Cynthia Irwin-Williams, principal investigator for the San Juan Valley Archaeological Project (aka the Salmon Ruins Project). © Salmon Ruins Museum.

The Great Houses at Aztec, Built to Last

Gary M. Brown

Today we call them great houses. We don't know what the people who created these buildings called them, but we can be sure they considered them great. They were supposed to amaze you. Aztec welcomed congregations of guests who marveled at the monumental buildings; today, after centuries of harsh weather and neglect, we still admire the elegant masonry walls towering more than two stories in height (fig. 4.1). The structures at Aztec Ruins National Monument have aged well—original wall features and roofs on dozens of rooms have survived—and still do what they were intended to do. They fill us with awe and respect for the people who designed and constructed such a spectacular civic center with stones, mud, and wood. These extraordinary people built at least four imposing structures that archaeologists classify as great houses, situated amid numerous additional public, ceremonial, and residential buildings forming a well-organized layout (fig. 4.2).

Great houses were built in the open, sometimes in prominent places that bear the full brunt of weather and erosion, yet they have stood up for centuries (fig. 4.3). Their exceptional state of preservation is not accidental. A dedicated preservation crew employed by the National Park Service wages a constant battle against deterioration of the ruins, working to arrest their destruction, but the struggle is hopeful because the great houses were made to endure. Most Pueblo people at this time lived in small, modest houses that might last a generation or two, but the great houses were constructed to outlast their builders (fig. 4.4). After many centuries, however, stabilizing the ruins and preserving them for future generations is a challenge that requires constant attention (fig. 4.5).

The inhabitants departed more than seven centuries ago. These majestic structures have since astonished countless visitors: early Navajos who called this area home after the Ancestral Pueblo people had left; Spanish explorers several centuries later; Anglo homesteaders in the late 1800s CE, who thought the great houses might have been built by the Aztecs of Mexico; archaeologists excavating the ruins in the early 1900s; and contemporary townsfolk and visitors to the town of Aztec, New Mexico. We have all been struck by the grandeur of these enormous geometric buildings and the urban landscape situated in an otherwise ordinary river valley winding from snowcapped peaks in the Rocky Mountains across the arid mesa country of northwestern New Mexico. The planned community provides a remarkable contrast to the natural beauty of the Animas Valley.

The great houses were designed to impress people as powerful symbols of human achievement and adaptation to the natural environment. The Animas River provided water for irrigation most of the time, washed out farms during occasional floods, then dropped too low to flow into canals during dry years. People needed options to survive the long haul, and one option would have been storing surplus food in big communal structures like the great houses at Aztec. The scale of construction and the economy of scale at that time had not previously been seen in the Middle San Juan region. People worked together in cohesive groups to achieve common goals that exceeded what smaller groups before them had accomplished. They intended for these impressive monuments to hold up for generations.

Aztec in its heyday was an extensive series of monumental buildings within a formal architectural landscape

Figure 4.1. The view from the third story at Aztec West looks over kivas and other mid-twelfth-century architectural renovations. The rooftops of these structures provided elevated courtyards overlooking the great central plaza. Courtesy of the National Park Service, Gary Brown, photographer.

Gary M. Brown

Figure 4.2. Excavations by the American Museum of Natural History in the eastern portion of the great house at Aztec West, 1920. This pioneering project demonstrated the status of Aztec as a major outlier site closely related to the great houses at Chaco Canyon. Courtesy of the Division of Anthropology, American Museum of Natural History (AMNH library image no. 119620), photographer unknown.

Figure 4.3. Excavations by the National Park Service in the western portion of the great house at Aztec West, 2010. This project succeeded in reducing the huge weight and pressure of unexcavated portions of the site on pueblo walls that had been exposed by previous excavations in the early twentieth century. Courtesy of the National Park Service, Joel Gamache, photographer.

that made a statement about the shared identity of people in the community and the visitors who joined them periodically for ceremonial gatherings and social interaction. The architecture spoke eloquently about who these people were and their relationship to the great society of Chaco Canyon. The ruins persist as a legacy of magnificent achievements in the distant past. This legacy comes alive when Pueblo Indians conduct ceremonies or social dances at Zuni, Acoma, and other modern pueblos. Such traditions cement kin, marriage, and ceremonial relationships; help to sustain a way of life and beliefs; and connect Pueblo people with their past. The antiquity of these traditions can be appreciated by those who visit the ruins at Aztec and imagine what might have happened when people came together to celebrate the summer solstice or a potluck feast in the year 1120.

At that time, Aztec had taken center stage in the Middle San Juan. A coordinated group of local folks and Chacoan migrants had almost finished the largest great house ever constructed outside Chaco Canyon. They had been working on the western great house at Aztec for more than a decade, surpassing Salmon in the monumental scale of construction. Aztec was at its peak! People at Salmon had enjoyed comparable status for several years, but their endeavor was just nearing

completion when groundbreaking began at Aztec West, less than ten miles away. The ideas were similar—a huge rectangular roomblock with wings at either end to embrace a spacious plaza. A large elevated structure within the central roomblock helped form an overall E shape when viewed from above. Someone standing on the roof of this elevated kiva could look over the plaza. Adjacent rooftops on the first, second, and third stories formed elevated courtyards that also faced the plaza below. Large groups could assemble and hold ceremonies in the plaza, while smaller groups could congregate on the rooftops connected to suites of rooms housing individual kin groups.

By 1120 the builders at Aztec West had produced a gigantic three-storied central block of rooms with a perpendicular wing on the east side of the plaza. A similar wing on the west side was nearly complete. They placed a smaller arc of connected rooms on the south side of the plaza beyond the great kiva. Thus, the essential plan might be described as a D shape. Multiple stories ascending from the level of the plaza arranged the rooftop courtyards into terraces that dropped off abruptly at the back, with sheer walls that dropped thirty feet to the ground. The architects aligned the back wall of the great house so that the sun on both the morning of the summer solstice and the evening of the winter solstice cast a

Figure 4.4. Mechanized backfilling of some areas at Aztec West has helped to preserve many tall and fragile walls, especially multistory architecture that once stood three and perhaps even four stories high in the northern roomblock. Multiple conveyors in this photograph carry fill dirt from the hopper at far right, outside the great house, into the room at left. Backfilling restored equilibrium to much of the site that had been exposed by the previous excavations. Courtesy of the National Park Service, Brian Culpepper, photographer.

Figure 4.5. The ancient masonry at Aztec Ruins is maintained by a skilled crew of preservationists who try to replicate ancient masonry styles as they stabilize deteriorating architecture. Courtesy of the National Park Service, Gary Brown, photographer.

glimmer of light down the long, tall rear wall. A balcony extending from this wall furnished the ideal place to witness the solstice events, though only a limited number of people could have assembled in these prime spots.

My research and collaboration with other authors in this book provide evidence that Aztec West, like Salmon Pueblo, served as a colony to institute and maintain close ties with Chaco Canyon. Chacoan migrants who had been instrumental in planning and building Aztec had formed an influential segment of the local society. Were they in charge? Some archaeologists think so; some even believe they were royalty. Others, including myself, don't see Aztec and Salmon as the kind of colonies that ruled over the local population. The leaders relied more on specialized knowledge and vibrant ceremonies than

institutional authority and hereditary power. They did not coerce other people. Chacoan migrants intermarried with the local populace; their descendants had kinship and other social ties with people in both Chaco Canyon and the Animas Valley. Aztec was thus the center of a complex multicultural society that perpetuated the Chacoan legacy and at the same time mixed it with local traditions to create an exciting new future for later generations.

Unlike at Salmon, many people lived near Aztec before Chacoan migrants colonized the Middle San Juan. Archaeological surveys identify Aztec as an important center of population by the middle of the eleventh century, a time when great houses stretched for miles through Chaco Canyon, yet only a few "outlier" sites at key points around the San Juan Basin reveal affinities with Chaco. Despite Chaco's profound influence, most people were content to build their own homes in everyday vernacular style, depending on resources that were readily available, the family labor pool, and skills learned from parents and grandparents. The local inhabitants of the Animas Valley commonly used river cobbles and adobe for the walls of their dwellings. Some early pueblos were bigger than would have been necessary, even by the standards of the largest extended families, and possibly represent the cooperative efforts of lineages consisting of related families. However, even large groups of related families could not have built the great houses at Chaco Canyon during the eleventh century and slightly later at Salmon and Aztec.

As many as a thousand people lived in the urban landscape that extended for about a mile around Aztec by the early 1100s. Hundreds of additional people inhabited villages nearby, as well as rural areas between villages. Farmers tilled cornfields up and down the Animas Valley on both sides of the river, and a variety of irrigation, floodwater, and dry-farming systems were managed as community enterprises. Aztec may have served as a communal center where leaders collected and stored surplus crops, which they could give back to hungry people in times of need. Aztec was the hub of social, economic, political, and religious affairs.

Two or three decades before beginning work on the western great house, the people of Aztec had constructed an adobe building that was the largest pueblo of the time. They placed Aztec North on a mesa overlooking the Animas River in the midst of a growing community, which consisted of numerous small "unit pueblos" and some larger buildings. The D-shaped pueblo at Aztec North contained a plaza and a large kiva where residents and neighbors could congregate. This type of layout, with an arc of rooms enclosing the plaza, was common at Chaco Canyon and foreshadowed the footprint of Aztec West. Aztec North was built in the 1060s or 1070s, when Chacoan migrants had just begun to colonize the Middle San Juan area and before the great houses at Salmon or Aztec West had been constructed. The people who built Aztec North were probably local folks who had participated in gatherings at Chaco Canyon; they attempted to

replicate the great houses they had seen, using construction techniques more familiar to them.

The builders of Aztec North used construction techniques unlike those of Chaco Canyon, where great houses had been made with sandstone masonry since their beginning in the ninth century. The locals at Aztec instead relied on techniques and materials that they were accustomed to, but their building looked just like a Chacoan great house—massive, multistoried, geometric, situated in a planned setting, located alongside a road, and further demarcated by rock berms, retaining walls, and earthen mounds that focused attention toward the center of a sweeping architectural landscape. From the outside, the central structure would have looked the same as a masonry great house because the last step in pueblo construction was plastering, even when this protective coat obscured meticulous masonry handiwork. I believe that Aztec North was an attempt by people in the Animas Valley to construct a community center like the great houses they had seen on visits to Chaco Canyon. Chaco was a vital center of religion and social activity, attracting pilgrims and traders from across the Four Corners area. People far and wide were inspired by Chaco. Its greatness was something to emulate.

By the end of the eleventh century, Chacoan colonization of the Middle San Juan was well under way with construction of the great house at Salmon. People from Chaco migrated to Salmon and slightly later to Aztec, where grand aspirations were beginning to materialize at Aztec West. Salmon and Aztec West not only appeared similar to classic Chacoan great houses; the details of their construction reflect close ties between the people of Salmon, Aztec, and Chaco (fig. 4.6). The original excavators at Salmon and Aztec thought migrants from Chaco had built the great houses, an assumption supported by recent archaeological research. The idea that we propose here and elsewhere in this book is that people from Chaco Canyon established colonies at both places in the 1090s and early 1100s. Although population movements throughout and beyond the Middle San Juan were dynamic and fluid, we use the term *colony* to describe large-scale movement into an occupied area to establish a base of operations for people who maintained strong links to the motherland. Rather than assimilate,

Gary M. Brown

Figure 4.6. This kiva on the second story at Aztec West is part of the initial Chacoan great house that was built in the early 1100s. The first story beneath it was filled in to support the elevated structure. Courtesy of the National Park Service, Gary Brown, photographer.

migrants from Chaco brought new ways of doing things and the knowledge required to do them.

How did local folks feel about colonization? We can't say for sure, but they probably welcomed these migrants since they already were closely aligned. Like many people from far and wide, inhabitants of the Middle San Juan made periodic visits to Chaco Canyon for large gatherings and sacred observances. People had adopted Chacoan religious beliefs, and local architects were building modest versions of great houses like those appearing throughout the San Juan Basin. Folks at Aztec in the late eleventh century were already emulating the extravagant architecture that had made Chaco famous. Why not welcome priests, leaders, architects, and master craftsmen from the greatest place that people had seen?

The leaders at Aztec might even have recruited Chacoan expertise, because the adobe-walled northern great house had probably started to sag after a few decades. The people of Aztec may have looked to Chaco

for a chance to enhance their status when the colony at Salmon assumed its role as the largest town in the Middle San Juan. But Salmon's distinction as the main regional center was brief. Its construction was still under way when a new group of Chacoan migrants and Aztec locals broke ground at Aztec West. To lay the foundations of the great house, they had to level masonry walls from previous work, possibly an earlier attempt at emulating great-house construction. Little is known about this predecessor except that it represents the first efforts of people at Aztec to shape sandstone blocks so masons could manufacture thick, sturdy walls that could support monumental architecture better than adobe. The razed walls might have been part of an unfinished building that was in the way of a big idea.

By 1120 this big idea stood at least three stories tall and had more than four hundred spacious rooms with high ceilings, which were more comparable to the rooms we live in today than those in most neighboring pueblos.

The walls were three feet thick and had a carefully crafted sandstone veneer on both faces and rough sandstone masonry in the middle. This core-veneer masonry technique was characteristic of classic Chacoan construction and enabled the great-house builders to create strong load-bearing walls. The builders at Aztec West employed techniques that would have required specialized training, such as laying core-veneer masonry, tying walls together with internal wooden rods, and building walls on cobble-filled trenches that provided foundations suitable for multistory architecture. Visitors who saw the great house after construction was finished would not have seen these details. If they tried to emulate this type of construction, they would have done so without the benefit of such specialized knowledge.

The team of archaeologists who performed detailed architectural documentation at Aztec Ruins under my direction was able to observe these subtle aspects of wall construction and technological style. We worked alongside preservation experts who routinely repaired damaged walls and frequently had to dismantle them in order to correct problems caused by deterioration. Such necessarily invasive preservation techniques made it possible for us to observe the internal characteristics and to learn how walls and roofs had been constructed. We were also able to learn details about how task groups organized their construction activities, alternating between veneer and core stonework, masonry walls and wooden roof assembly, or wrapping up one day's work and tying it into the next day's construction. We found many examples of superb masonry veneers with thin sandstone chinking (chinking stones are small stones used to level masonry during the construction process), which we believe reflect classic Chacoan craftsmanship learned from masters who had been trained at Chaco Canyon. We also documented walls that showed the kind of variation in skill level and style that might be expected from master and apprentice working side by side as they laid up courses of masonry walls.

We learned a great deal about the logistics and processes of great house construction from the subtle architectural characteristics that reflect technological style, conventions, and habits learned from others. We depend heavily on this type of analysis to determine whether architecture was produced by locals using their traditional vernacular, or migrants using techniques typical of sites elsewhere. The intimate details of great-house construction at Aztec West are so similar to those documented by previous studies and observations at Chaco Canyon that we can best explain the similarities, many of them clear departures from traditional local practices, as the result of experienced craftspeople trained at and most likely from Chaco. We see many additional aspects of the construction effort that suggest Chacoan experts and leaders. The rapid pace of large-scale construction is one example, unprecedented in the Middle San Juan until Aztec West and Salmon were built in a total span of about thirty-five years.

The master architects, planners, and leaders from Chaco Canyon demanded the best construction materials when they and the local inhabitants embarked on construction of the western great house at Aztec. They needed large quantities of rock that was suitable for coursed masonry. Local river cobbles were good enough to build ordinary dwellings, but not the great house. Quarry workers hauled sandstone several miles from the best sources in quantities that make my back ache just contemplating the task. They selected special varieties of stone for unique masonry features, such as majestic greenstone stripes along the western facade.

Timber crews made countless trips to harvest and transport pine, fir, spruce, aspen, and other trees from forests more than twenty-five miles away. They covered rooms and circular kivas with wooden roofs that were supported by timbers the size of telephone poles. By 1120, after about two-thirds of the great house had been finished, the builders had lowered their standards and workers commonly made shorter trips to piñon and juniper woodlands closer to Aztec. Despite the abundance of juniper in the immediate area, people still traveled ten miles or more to higher elevations where juniper and piñon trees with straight, uniform trunks were more common and could be more easily cut to standard proportions. By this time, roofers were substituting two or three juniper beams for one pine or spruce log. As work progressed through the west wing, the builders reduced the size of rooms in order to make such compromises feasible.

Numerous specialized craftspeople worked together on this huge enterprise. Experienced specialists with

Figure 4.7. Large kivas in the central roomblock at Aztec West that were built into a renovated area where earlier habitation rooms were partially dismantled to accommodate the larger kivas during twelfth-century reorganization of the great house. Excavators are clearing the corners of the former habitation rooms after the kivas themselves had been excavated. © University of Colorado Museum of Natural History, photographer unknown.

refined skills in woodworking and framing windows and doorways had clearly learned their trade at Chaco Canyon. Such masters served as mentors who worked closely with local apprentices to instruct them in the fine points of Chacoan construction. Overall, the work seems to have been very well coordinated, yet many attributes of the architecture, masonry, and roofs have led me to the conclusion that the eastern half of the building was constructed and occupied largely by Chacoan migrants, and the western half primarily by local inhabitants of the Animas Valley. Local folks who occupied the western half of Aztec West might have moved from the earlier great house at Aztec North. The western half even has examples of thick adobe walls adjacent to typical Chacoan core-veneer masonry.

The circular kivas at Aztec provided important venues for ceremonial life both in the privacy of the interiors and in public on top of the flat roofs that served as courtyards. Priests could control access to the inside of a kiva, normally entered via a ladder through a hatch in the roof, but once on the rooftop, participants performed ceremonies in view of congregations gathered together at the great house. As originally constructed and occupied at 1120, Aztec West had only a few kivas, but they were

large. An elevated central kiva within the roomblock and an even larger great kiva in the plaza were situated along the axis that divides Aztec West into halves (fig. 4.7). Doorways connected the top of the central kiva with rooftop courtyards to the east and west, suggesting that people from both sides participated in ceremonial activities linked to this important space. The east and west sides of the great house each contained another large kiva that was more exclusive and probably focused activities within that half of the site. However, the great kiva and plaza would have served to integrate people at Aztec West with other groups in the Animas Valley by drawing large numbers of people together for ceremonies, feasting, trade, and social interaction.

Aztec West dominated the scene by 1120, but other large villages and smaller pueblos throughout the Animas Valley helped the community thrive by providing homes for farmers who utilized an extensive system of irrigation canals to produce staples for the local population and even exports for Chaco Canyon. In the midst of all this, another gigantic project was initiated at Aztec East. Unlike Aztec West, with a southeast-facing passive-solar orientation, the new great house was laid out in accordance with the cardinal directions and faced south.

Figure 4.8. The Hubbard Tri-Wall structure at Aztec Ruins National Monument, with the central kiva surrounded by concentric rows of rooms. Courtesy of the National Park Service, George Schweier, photographer.

Like Aztec West, it had a very tall, sheer wall at the back and stepped down in terraces toward the front, with the doorways from the upper stories opening onto rooftops that overlooked an expansive plaza and great kiva.

Ultimately, Aztec East would approach its predecessor in size, but the construction crews initially concentrated on a rectangular roomblock with a large aboveground kiva surrounded on all sides by multistory rooms. Aztec East would eventually consist of two large rectangular roomblocks separated by a narrow walkway that connected the main plaza toward the front with a series of smaller structures and yet another large great house behind it. Halfway between Aztec East and Aztec West stood a huge circular structure with an elevated kiva in the middle and three concentric rows of rooms fully

encircling the kiva. This structure is unique, although Aztec also has variations of this type of multiwalled structure with two concentric rows, or just one row, of rooms. Archaeologists sometimes call the first type a "tri-wall" and the second a "bi-wall" to describe the circular walls encircling the kiva. The people at Chaco built a single tri-wall at Pueblo del Arroyo, but the size and number of such multiwalled structures is exceptional. This suggests to me that multiwalled structures at Aztec might represent an innovation where collaboration between local and Chacoan builders provided a fertile environment for architectural evolution (fig. 4.8).

Aztec must have been a bustling construction site in 1120, with the western great house almost completed, major work on the eastern great house under way, and

Gary M. Brown

construction of numerous additional buildings showing distinctive varieties of Chacoan masonry and architectural style. Can you imagine the stockpiles of building supplies? Not long after 1120, while construction at Aztec East was gearing up, the inhabitants of Aztec West began a major renovation. They converted several residential room suites into large kivas and added modest-sized rooms in other areas. To make way for the new kivas, they dismantled massive walls and blocked doorways that previously had led into additional rooms toward the back of the building. The purpose of this huge renovation effort is not obvious, but people certainly had new ideas about how the site should be organized. They still used the four original kivas, including the great kiva, but they wanted more kivas and a greater proportion of kivas to other rooms.

The new pattern is characteristic throughout the construction of Aztec East. People built more kivas, generally quite large, while other rooms were smaller than those typical of the western great house, though still larger than common pueblos at other sites. Construction of the eastern great house was organized into discrete sections instead of one gigantic, unified plan. This trend toward compartmentalized construction with more numerous kivas progressed throughout the twelfth

century as people carried out additional renovations at Aztec West and kept adding new room suites onto the initial nucleus at Aztec East. New construction elsewhere in the Middle San Juan and renovations at other great houses, such as at Salmon (see chapter 3), was characterized by even greater proportions of kivas to other rooms, but these kivas were considerably smaller than those built during the reorganization of Aztec West and new construction at Aztec East (fig. 4.9).

I conclude from this trend that society became more segmented after the initial influx of Chacoan colonists, though the segments were still larger than ordinary family households. In fact, many large residential room suites at Aztec West were reorganized into even larger arrangements of rooms oriented around sizable kivas. This change suggests that parts of the town were dedicated to ceremonial groups whose members, like those in modern Puebloan societies, did not necessarily live together near the kiva. These kiva groups drew members from throughout the great house and potentially beyond, thereby helping to integrate the growing population. The renovation made it harder to divide Aztec West into halves reflecting local and migrant populations. The continuing progress on Aztec East made such divisions even harder to draw. The great house emerging there had

Figure 4.9. Room suites at Aztec East dating to the 1200s were connected to this habitation room. The architecture has both Chacoan attributes and unique features, which include this D-shaped fire hearth (note straight side on lower left edge) and raised doorway with sill constructed of wooden poles embedded in the wall. Courtesy of the National Park Service, Cheryl Paddock, photographer.

a modular layout related to incremental construction, but the layout also appears to reflect a more segmented social organization. People built suites of rooms focused on a particular kiva that was elevated well above ground level, and surrounding rooms on higher stories enclosed a courtyard, obscured from public view, situated on the roof of the kiva. Thus, people at Aztec in the middle and late twelfth century seem to have been organized into kiva groups, with ten or more such groups at each of the major great houses.

This was the post-Chacoan era. Soon after 1120, the greatest of the great houses at Chaco Canyon had been built, people were migrating from Chaco to destinations in all directions, and Chacoan society was beginning to unravel. The torch had been passed to Aztec, where people had hit their stride. The scale of influence tipped from Aztec West to Aztec East as the twelfth century unfolded, and by the thirteenth century Aztec East assumed dominance as a thriving regional center. People kept adding new Chacoan-style room suites onto the eastern great house and introducing new kinds of masonry and architectural features that gave the old canons a fresh twist. They kept Chacoan traditions alive by continually building onto a unique great house that enshrined this vital part of their past. They constructed major additions onto upper stories of the great house into the middle of the thirteenth century.

Meanwhile, the residents of Aztec West turned their attention toward the more usual vernacular architecture during the thirteenth century. They partitioned many of the original large rooms into small chambers, or converted square rooms into small kivas by constructing circular structures inside them or sometimes by simply rounding off corners (fig. 4.10). The earlier trend toward more numerous, smaller kivas escalated, resulting in dozens of units appropriate for household ceremonies at Aztec West, whereas sizable kiva groups at Aztec East continued to integrate larger segments in the social fabric of the community there. As time passed, the locals who had built and occupied the west half of the western great house once again reorganized the pueblo, even dismantling portions of the original building and using stones from the Chacoan masonry to construct simple domiciles alongside the great house. Many of these domiciles

resemble the unit pueblos that had been typical of the Animas and surrounding areas throughout the Chacoan and post-Chacoan eras.

The occupants of Aztec East maintained the Chacoan legacy for more than a century after the collapse of Chaco Canyon itself. They built additional Chacoan-style roomblocks well into the thirteenth century and cut beams in 1269 to support a sagging roof in a portion of the great house constructed by their ancestors a century and a half earlier. No tree-ring samples date any later than this. I assume that people left soon after the roof was repaired, because later pottery types are absent from Aztec and other Middle San Juan sites. The people of Salmon Pueblo replaced the roof of their great kiva at about the same time, but again we have no evidence of subsequent occupation into the late thirteenth century or beyond. The Middle San Juan—including Aztec and Salmon—was subjected to the same widespread depopulation that was characteristic of the entire Four Corners area.

We know that a long drought and colder weather made high-desert farming difficult in the late thirteenth century. We also know that social unrest and other problems made life turbulent. Conflicts and even warfare appear to be related to environmental stress, but previous periods of tension between populations in the area had been resolved. Some archaeologists emphasize warfare and violence in their accounts of Chacoan and post-Chacoan occupations, but indications of violent conflict at Aztec are limited, small-scale events that can unfortunately be expected anywhere and anytime in human experience. The Chacoan way of life, with its emphasis on large multicultural gatherings, communal enterprises, and shared traditions, may have been instrumental in resolving such conflicts. By the mid-thirteenth century, however, Chaco Canyon was history and Aztec had become a provincial center surrounded by large, crowded villages that were relatively autonomous.

We do not fully understand why the inhabitants of Aztec left the Middle San Juan, especially those who had continued to invest so much in the eastern great house at Aztec. People were migrating throughout the Southwest, establishing towns even bigger than Aztec and Chaco in areas with better summer rainfall. Tens of thousands

Gary M. Brown

Figure 4.10. Test excavations at Aztec West in 2012 revealed a small kiva that had been built into an original Chacoan room suite during the 1200s. Many small kivas of this type were built into the original rooms of the great house during the thirteenth century. Courtesy of the National Park Service, Nicole Shurack, photographer.

of people who inhabited the Middle and Northern San Juan regions during the mid-thirteenth century began a series of migrations, joining distant neighbors on the Rio Grande to the southeast, on the Hopi Mesas to the southwest, and across the large area in between. The simultaneous attraction of these new places, the growing towns reminiscent of the glory days at Aztec and Chaco, and deteriorating conditions in the Four Corners may have triggered the exodus, but large-scale population movements from such a vast area remain hard to explain.

EARL MORRIS AT AZTEC RUINS

Earl Morris was a pioneer in Southwestern archaeology. His work at Aztec is just one of his many accomplishments. He trained Aztec farm workers to excavate and employed skilled masons to stabilize the fragile walls so that digging could be done safely. They loaded railroad cars with artifacts destined for New York City. The American Museum of Natural History sponsored the excavation and donated the site to the National Park Service in 1924 after excavating two hundred rooms.

Morris collaborated with Andrew Douglass at the University of Arizona in the first archaeological application of tree-ring dating. They sampled beams from intact roofs at Aztec West, as well as Pueblo Bonito at Chaco Canyon. Although the prehistoric tree-ring sequence would not be correlated to our modern calendar until later, Douglass was able to correlate overlapping tree rings from the two sites and show that Pueblo Bonito was built earlier. Subsequent work by many collectors at Aztec West has produced the largest sample of tree-ring dates from any Southwestern site, but the initial specimens established the basic fact that allowed Morris to speculate that great-house architecture originated at Chaco Canyon and was later introduced to Aztec by migrants from Chaco.

Morris also saw similarities between the earliest pottery at Aztec and the pottery found at Chaco. The striking resemblance in architecture and the tree-ring sequence provided by Douglass made it possible for Morris to hypothesize that Aztec was built by Chacoan migrants. However, since most pottery at Aztec was similar to that of Mesa Verde, Morris concluded that Chacoan people left Aztec, perhaps returning to Chaco Canyon, and that a second wave of people then reoccupied the site, this time migrating from Mesa Verde.

We now know that many of the various Mesa Verde traits noted by Morris appeared just as early or even earlier at Aztec. Many of us today doubt that Aztec was abandoned and reoccupied after a period of disuse. We discern continuities that are consistent with culture change and social reorganization. Nevertheless, our current ideas are founded upon the initial facts and inferences that comprise the legacy of Earl Morris.

Gary M. Brown

Aztec West's Great Kiva

Florence C. Lister

Hollywood could not have dreamed up a character who better epitomized the popular perception of an archaeologist than Earl Morris. Rumor had it that the costume of fictional archaeologist Indiana Jones was based upon a photograph of this real-life archaeologist who worked during the last decades of the nineteenth century and the first decades of the twentieth in the northern Southwest, specifically the San Juan Basin.

This basin was sliced in half, more or less, by the San Juan River as it rushed to merge with the Colorado River and what is now Lake Powell. The land north of the river was more elevated and more verdant than the land to the south and had many more sources of water. This vast area was Earl's home turf. Seemingly empty, the central portion of this province was not occupied by whites until after the Civil War, when settlers arrived intent on taking up tracts of land and taming the wilderness.

As the settlers began clearing and developing their land, they encountered the remains of what appeared to have once been domestic structures and work areas, which they erroneously attributed to the Aztec Indians. The settlers called a group of ruins along the west side of the Animas River "Aztec" and repeated that designation so often that it became the proper name for what turned out to be the largest complex of ruins in the middle San Juan Valley (see chapter 4).

Groups of men, including Scott Morris, father of Earl, soon began scouting the valley for trophies. When not busy hauling freight to mining camps in the La Plata Mountains, Scott would bundle up Earl and take off for a day of exploring the valleys just north of Farmington, New Mexico. Like most toddlers, Earl enjoyed digging in the dirt, and he later remembered that at the age of three

he unearthed what turned out to be the bowl of a dipper. This vessel was the first in what became his large collection of Ancestral Pueblo pottery.

After graduating from high school in Farmington, Earl enrolled at the University of Colorado in Boulder. There, he secured a student job at the university museum, where for the first time he encountered adults who were seriously interested in the prehistory of their state. These scholars, impressed with Earl's knowledge of the antiquities in his home area, paid him during two summer vacations to find pottery that they could add to the museum collections.

Earl first visited Aztec Ruins with his father; he returned in 1915 accompanied by Nels Nelson, staff archaeologist for the American Museum of Natural History in New York. When Nelson returned to New York, he recommended that the museum sponsor an excavation of the westernmost of Aztec's two mounds—which was later called Aztec West and was the least disturbed—and he also recommended that Earl Morris be made the director of this excavation. Thus began Earl's long and illustrious career.

My husband, Robert Lister (longtime National Park Service archaeologist and author), and I developed a relationship with Earl Morris and his second wife, Lucille, at informal social gatherings. Although always treated as an honored guest, Earl stayed in the background and almost never mentioned his many adventures in archaeology. However, Bob had one very memorable personal experience with Earl.

One summer day, as Bob and Earl drove from Boulder to attend a regional archaeology conference, Earl suggested that they briefly stop at Aztec Ruins. As soon

Figure 5.1. The great kiva at Aztec West after excavation by the American Museum of Natural History in 1921. Masonry remnants forming the bases of the four pillars that supported the roof, large vaults adjacent to the two nearest pillars, and a large masonry fire hearth between them are all visible. © University of Colorado Museum of Natural History, Earl Morris, photographer.

as they parked, Earl walked directly to the great kiva. The men stood at the entrance for a few moments, awestruck, as most folks are, by the size and atmosphere of this sanctuary (fig. 5.1). Then Earl turned abruptly to Bob and said that he had solid evidence for everything he had done to reconstruct this building. Bob was rather taken aback, not understanding what Earl meant. As they worked their way through the ruin, Earl kept mumbling to himself about the great kiva. Later, when the men continued on their journey, Bob came to understand what it was that had Earl so agitated. Earl had learned that some of his colleagues were expressing doubts about the reliability of his work at the great kiva, which greatly upset him

because he considered it the crowning achievement of his long career (fig. 5.2).

Earl felt that these critics were implying that the Ancestral Pueblo people didn't have the mental or physical capacity to envision such a structure as the great kiva. He felt his Pueblo friends were being insulted. He couldn't understand why these doubters wouldn't put their prejudices aside and view the Ancestral Pueblo people as favorably as he did. After a while, however, Earl relaxed, as though he had let go of a heavy burden, and then he apologized to Bob for his rant. As for Bob, he felt humbled that this very important man had felt comfortable enough to express his concerns. During the

Florence C. Lister

rest of their journey, Earl continued to think about the great kiva and went on to share with Bob some of his recollections.

Earl said that when the American Museum of Natural History so abruptly and unexpectedly terminated excavation at Aztec Ruins in 1921, he was despondent because he felt he had not finished his job. The west wing of the structure was only partially opened up, and he wanted to have the whole structure cleared. Furthermore, he didn't know what his future would hold, and he had his mother to support. Just after 1921, upon termination of work at Aztec, he eagerly accepted an invitation to join three colleagues—pioneering archaeologists Neil Judd, Sylvanus "Vay" Morley, and Alfred "Ted" Kidder—on a two-day wagon trip down to Chaco Canyon. The men spent several days investigating the ruins scattered along the Chaco Wash and most of their time at Pueblo Bonito, the largest of all the structures in Chaco,

which had been partially excavated during four seasons between 1896 and 1901.

One afternoon, as they were loitering around Pueblo Bonito, their conversation turned to the obvious importance that the Ancestral Pueblo people placed on religious ceremonialism. Every dwelling, large or small, had at least one chamber set aside for such purposes. Such chambers were called kivas: circular structures with complex traditional features. These small structures would accommodate only a few people at any one time. But the archaeologists at Pueblo Bonito went on to discuss the much larger rooms (later identified as great kivas) that also seemed to have been set aside for ceremonial activities. None of them had been excavated, though they were associated with almost all of the great houses, and Earl hadn't really thought about them before.

On the way back to Aztec, Earl got to wondering if there wasn't another type of kiva at Aztec West.

Figure 5.2. The National Park Service reconstructing the Aztec great kiva as part of a Public Works Administration project in 1934. Earl Morris led the project and assisted with design of the reconstructed building. Courtesy of the National Park Service, photographer unknown, possibly George Grant.

He thought about a noticeable depression off the east wing of the building. Like a crater, it collected a muddy pool of water in its center after every summer shower, and he had often wondered if something interesting might be buried there. Earl had been too busy finishing up his work at the great house to explore this depression, but the more he thought about it, the depression was in exactly the right location to contain such a structure. So as soon as he got back to Aztec, he wrote a letter to the museum staff in New York asking for permission to investigate the depression, even though the Aztec West project had been formally terminated.

In due time, the museum responded favorably. Earl was especially eager to get to work because he thought that Neil Judd was about to finish his excavation at Pueblo Bonito (work that actually took Judd another seven seasons). He regarded Judd as a friend but also a rival, and he said he was downright jealous when he learned that the National Geographic Society planned to sponsor Judd, which meant that his work would be generously funded as well as publicized in the society's widely distributed magazine.

Earl recalled that in February 1921, while the ground was still partially frozen, he asked a few of the local men who had worked with him on Aztec's great house to come and help excavate the depression. Within a month, despite the unfavorable conditions, these men and Earl had cleaned it out. As he looked over the excavation, Earl must have said to himself, "Yes, this is my variant kiva," and he was thrilled with the idea that he might be the very first person to report on such a structure. Earl referred to this structure as a great kiva, and in time *great kiva* became the proper term for this type of construction.

What Earl saw after the excavation was a very large chamber that had been cut at least nineteen feet below the ground's surface and forty-eight feet across at its widest point. Encircling the depression on the surface were small rooms, twelve in number when they were first constructed but increased to fifteen during remodeling. The surface rooms were obviously an integral part of the great kiva, and each had a door to the exterior. On the opposite wall of each room, the builders had knocked

an opening into the central chamber and inserted a very narrow pole ladder into a slot that led from the room down to a bench that encircled the entire great kiva. Earl speculated that these chambers were meant to be dressing rooms, where participants in various rituals could change their costumes as required. Subsequent investigations have shown that surface-level rooms encircling the main chamber of a great kiva are unique to Aztec.

Four low walls that formed a cube four feet high had been built on the floor of the great kiva. A compacted deposit of ashes and cinders filled the bottom of the cube. Obviously, many fires had been maintained in this enclosed hearth. A pair of large rectangular units several feet high had also been built on the floor. Like the structure itself, they were aligned north–south, but their purpose is unknown. Earl speculated, as others have also done, that Ancestral Pueblo people laid planking over these units and that performers on top of the planks made noises with their feet, which resounded through the chamber. In other words, these could have been foot drums.

Many, many pieces of partially burned wood and charcoal lay scattered throughout the fill of the structures. At some unknown time, what must have been a catastrophic fire had raged in the north end of this great kiva, scorching and discoloring walls and so hardening plasters that they peeled off in showers of flakes. A sizable section of the roof had collapsed more or less as a unit, and the impressions of the logs that formed the framework of the roof were left in the dirt floor of the great kiva, which aided Earl in drafting a plan of the roof's framework. His meticulous study of the impressions allowed him to create an accurate plan that later aided reconstruction of the great kiva (fig. 5.3).

Earl had been concerned all along with whether the surface rooms had been roofed independently of the main chamber. This arrangement would have required a great deal more labor and raw materials, and if they had been independently constructed, the roofs of the surface rooms would have been at least fifteen feet higher than the roof over the central chamber. Precipitation falling on the roofs of those rooms would inevitably have drained off onto the lower roof of the central chamber, causing a

Figure 5.3. Cutting roof beams for reconstructing the Aztec great kiva. The beams were set on top of the four masonry pillars inside the kiva and provide the main support for numerous secondary poles on which the earthen roof was laid. © University of Colorado Museum of Natural History, photographer unknown, 1934.

variety of structural problems. So Earl dismissed the idea of independent roofs on the surface rooms.

Earl's plan of the roof showed that very stout timbers had been laid from the top of one supporting column to the top of an adjacent column to form a square in the center of the great kiva. When Earl saw them, the remains of these supporting columns were still about three feet high. In most great kivas, the builders used evergreen trunks to support the roofs, but these would not have sufficed for the Aztec great kiva, because, Earl estimated, the roof would have been at least sixteen feet higher off the floor and would have weighed about nine tons.

Some very substantial support would have been necessary, and the columns in the Aztec great kiva were constructed in an ingenious fashion. First, the builders layered horizontal slabs of sandstone on the floor of the kiva. On top of the slabs they placed a layer of closely spaced, peeled logs in the opposite direction. They topped the logs with another layer of sandstone slabs, again laid in the opposite direction. The builders contin-ued to layer slabs and logs throughout the height of the

columns, then faced them with adobe plaster. This kind of construction gave the columns a little bit of flexibility to accommodate a slight shifting of the roof and demon-strated to Earl the ingenuity of the Ancestral Pueblo people.

Beneath each column the builders stacked four circular slabs of limestone to keep the columns from sinking farther into the soil. The nearest source for this limestone is thought to have been more than one hundred miles distant. Securing this resource would have been a monumental task because the builders had no conveyance with which to bring the slabs to Aztec; the ability to transport the limestone there is an indication of their industriousness and the reverence with which they viewed the great kiva.

After the excavation was completed, the site was left uncovered, and over the years heaps of tumbleweeds and windblown trash collected in the great kiva. It became so unsightly that the villagers living in the vicinity of Aztec began lobbying their congressional representatives to have the government clean it up. The American Museum of Natural History had deeded the property to the government in 1923, and Aztec Ruins was declared a national monument that same year and put under the jurisdiction of the National Park Service.

In time, the superintendent of the monument came up with a very bold idea: instead of just cleaning up the great kiva, why not totally reconstruct it? He argued that a reconstructed building would help visitors to better understand the ceremonial side of Ancestral Pueblo life. In 1934, at the depth of the Great Depression, the government made a substantial grant to the monument to be administered by the Works Progress Administration. Earl Morris was the logical choice for director of the project because he had overseen the original excavation thirteen years earlier.

Earl was most enthusiastic about the prospect of great-kiva reconstruction because of the kiva's advanced deterioration. However, he well knew that such an endeavor would include many opportunities for miscalculations, misconceptions, and mistakes. Some suggested that the great kiva was a religious structure significant to the Ancestral Pueblo and that any work on it should be done with proper reverence — that the restoration should reflect the workmanship of the Ancestral Pueblo people and the nature of their culture. Earl took these comments very much to heart. He saw the greatest challenge in the reconstruction as rebuilding the roof, which he knew would have been an even greater challenge for the original builders, who had to work without any mechanical help, including block and tackle, horses, metal tools, or even nails. Again, Earl felt justified in his high regard for their construction abilities.

Earl dispatched volunteers many miles up the Animas River Valley to the high San Juan Mountains and charged them to select suitable timbers with which to reconstruct the roof. These timbers had to be stout, straight, and lengthy and preferably of ponderosa pine.

Eventually, Earl reconstructed the great kiva so that the surface rooms were integrated with the subterranean chamber: the front walls of the surface rooms became the outside walls of the building. This method created one very large structure. However, Earl felt justified in this action because the slot ladders leading from the rooms down to the floor of the central chamber showed this arrangement to be the intention of the original builders.

As for the roof, Morris followed the plan he had worked out from the impression of the logs on the floor. Workers laid stout logs from the top of one column to the top of another, forming a square. Then they laid twenty-four additional logs across those beams so that one end of each reached the center of the square, rather like the hub of a wheel. Pairs of logs splayed out diagonally from there, like the spokes of a wagon wheel. These paired logs reached out to each of the surface rooms, so that both the surface rooms and the central chamber were covered by the framework of timbers. On top of this framework of logs, the workers laid a layer of vegetation, including willow branches and leaves, which they in turn covered with another layer of closely spaced, peeled log poles. They covered the whole business with a great quantity of earth, which filtered down between the little openings in these layers. When that earth got wet, of course, it turned to mud, and when that mud dried, it formed a very solid, compact mass holding everything together.

The massive roof transformed the great kiva into a monumental structure. This monumentality, which had been the objective of the original builders, shocked some observers, as did the height of the building, which was necessary in order to cover those surface rooms. Onlookers had not expected such a large structure, and they complained that this building would have overwhelmed the Ancestral Pueblo people instead of empowering them. But perhaps the original builders intended their great kiva to create just such a sense of awe.

As for Earl, he strongly believed that he and his crew had faithfully reproduced the original structure and that what observers saw in the twentieth century resembled what they would have seen in the twelfth, when the original kiva was built (fig. 5.4). He also rejected the idea that the Ancestral Pueblo people could not have appreciated its monumentality. He liked to think that they relished the spaciousness and loftiness of this theater, and he liked to envision what might have happened in the great kiva during the rituals that were held there.

Figure 5.4. The reconstructed great kiva and previously reconstructed court kiva in the plaza at Aztec West. Courtesy of the National Park Service, George Grant, photographer.

When people seated on the benches in the great kiva looked up and saw costumed figures descending from the surface-level rooms, they may have interpreted these figures as spirits from the supernatural world. An all-male chorus might have gathered in the great kiva to sing proper incantations for this particular ritual. Perhaps a flute sounded its mournful tune while dancers on top of the foot drums beat out a rhythm that united the whole affair, reaffirming for the witnesses their spiritual connection with the natural world.

In the years following, as the discipline of regional archaeology matured, archaeologists realized that rebuilding anything on a ruin was a mistake because of the danger of compromising the integrity of the original building. Similar reconstructions were completed at

Tuzigoot and Wupatki National Monuments in Arizona during the 1930s, but these were removed in the 1940s. Fortunately, the great kiva at Aztec was spared from destruction, partly because of the great expense it would have involved, but also because it was such an important addition not just to Aztec West, but to the Ancestral Pueblo record in general. In its unadorned condition and sparsely furnished with basic elements, it faithfully reflected the character of the Ancestral Pueblo people and gave future generations the opportunity to appreciate the importance of ceremony in the Ancestral Pueblo world.

Bob often thought of his unusual trip with Earl Morris, and he did so quite tearfully one Sunday when a telephone call informed him that Earl had died that

Figure 5.5. The Lister family inside Aztec West, 1987. *Left to right:* Frank Lister (son), Robert Lister, Florence Lister, and Gary Lister (son). Courtesy of Frank Lister.

morning while working in his rose garden in Boulder. It seemed rather fitting that he had his trusty, well-worn shovel in hand.

Bob was also quite concerned that the shadows of the controversy over the reconstruction of the great kiva would wrongfully dim the legacy of this outstanding homegrown scholar of the lower Animas Valley. Fortunately, this fear was never realized. Regardless of the controversy, however, the great kiva and Aztec Ruins in general are, in effect, memorials to this man. No other ruins site in the Southwest is so identified with one

individual as is Aztec West with Earl Morris. Even his ashes lie buried in the dirt floor of one of the undisclosed rooms he had excavated forty years earlier.

Editors' note: Florence Lister passed away on September 4, 2016, at the age of ninety-six. She lived an amazing life and made many, many contributions to American archaeology. We are honored to have this chapter, her final contribution to Southwest archaeology, in this volume.

Chacoan Archaeoastronomy of the Middle San Juan Region

Larry L. Baker

Over a thousand years ago, Chaco Canyon was the cultural center of a complex civilization previously unrivaled in North America. The inhabitants of this seemingly remote, windswept landscape constructed thirteen buildings, now known as great houses, along the margins of Chaco Wash and the mesas flanking the canyon. They became superb agriculturalists, growing corn, beans, squash, and perhaps a native cotton for textiles (see chapter 8). Concurrently, the timing of growing seasons and understanding of certain dates, such as the summer and winter solstices (the longest and shortest days of the year, respectively), became increasingly important to these intrepid farmers. This fundamental knowledge accrued over the centuries, and the need to mark specific times of the year with associated ritual activities gave rise to an incredible understanding of astronomy. In order to track seasonal and ceremonial cycles, the Pueblo people developed precise chronological devices: rock-art symbols pecked into cliff faces, as well as special features constructed within their great houses, on which they could observe the play of light and shadow created by the sun and moon on significant dates throughout the year.

Outlying communities, affiliated with Chaco at one level or another, sprang up around the San Juan Basin. Inhabitants of locales far from Chaco Canyon incorporated Chacoan architectural styles into their buildings, and "hallmarks" of Chacoan masonry allow archaeologists to distinguish Chacoan outliers from other prehistoric Puebloan sites across the region. By the late eleventh and early twelfth centuries, migrants from Chaco Canyon had moved into the San Juan, La Plata, and Animas River drainages, the region known as the Middle San

Juan. This area had previously seen minimal influence by Chacoan culture, and the immigrants brought all of the cultural traits of their forefathers with them, particularly their knowledge of monumental building construction. The Pueblo people incorporated specialized features into their new buildings, including elements related to astronomical observations. In this chapter, I explore Chacoan achievements in astronomy—what we now call archaeoastronomy, or the study of ancient astronomy—in the Middle San Juan region.

Archaeologists working in Chaco Canyon have proposed that its builders designed the site's geometry based in part on their astronomical observations and that this relationship between astronomy and architecture might be considered another hallmark of Chacoan buildings—a proposition that is supported by my recent research at Salmon Ruins. Salmon is located approximately forty-seven miles north of Chaco Canyon on the north bank of the San Juan River, about two miles west of Bloomfield, New Mexico. This Chacoan great house was constructed largely between 1088 and 1090 CE (fig. 6.1). As built, Salmon contained 275 rooms, three stories of construction in some areas, a central elevated kiva (ceremonial room), and a great kiva in the plaza for community-wide events (see chapter 3).

My initial work on the archaeoastronomy of Salmon began on the cold, crisp morning of December 21, 1997, the shortest day of the year. For several days, the sky had been overcast, and ultimately no observations were possible. My coresearcher, Kurt Mantonya, and I remained undaunted, however, and we continued our investigations on the summer solstice of 1998. We placed

Figure 6.1. An aerial photograph of Salmon Ruins taken during the last year of excavation, in 1978. © Salmon Ruins Museum, courtesy of Larry L. Baker, photographer.

targets in what we thought might be important positions related to astronomical alignments within a building's construction, for example, the centers of the great kiva and the Tower Kiva. As the sun rose in the distance but illuminated no magic tomb, à la *Raiders of the Lost Ark*, I shouted to my fellow observer, "This is bogus!"

Then I realized that the rising sun, the northeast corner of the pueblo, and a sandstone mosaic on the east wall of Room 59 were all aligned. I shot a compass bearing along this alignment, from the mosaic looking northeast, and wondered if this observation could be a coincidence; however, as I turned westward, I saw that the full moon was setting exactly opposite from where the sun was rising. I was struck by the sunrise and

moonset on opposite horizons, and I knew that Kurt and I should continue with our study of the relationship between astronomical alignments and the floor plan of the pueblo.

Over the next several years, we pinpointed key reference points in the pueblo's floor plan by observing select astronomical alignments. These key positions served as a one-to-one scale "blueprint" that could be laid directly over the alluvial terrace on which the pueblo was built. And we found that astronomical alignments related to summer and winter solstices, equinoxes, north-to-south cardinal alignments, and positions of the moon at the horizon were used by Salmon's ancient architects in their design of the pueblo (fig. 6.2).

Larry L. Baker

More recently, my research at Salmon Pueblo has focused on Room 82. This room is located in the building's central complex, adjacent to the Tower Kiva, and it was built during the Chacoan period. Several specialized features were built into the floor, and excavation of the room has indicated a nondomestic—and likely ceremonial—use. Brooks Marshall, a member of the San Juan County Museum Association, became intrigued with my archaeoastronomical interpretations of the room, in particular, its position facing the plaza, orientation toward the eastern sky, and astronomical observations made through a small window in the upper east wall. Marshall studied the detailed room records and determined that several features in the room could have facilitated astronomical observations. These features include a window in the east wall, a low adobe platform

along the northwest corner of the room, and a low, narrow wall in the room's interior that subdivided the floor space (fig. 6.3).

The window is located at the top of the room's east wall, just below the level of the ceiling. More than just a simple opening to the outside, the window had a masonry frame that was reduced in size with wooden slats and adobe mortar plastered against the masonry frame. A smoothed sandstone slab was set as the opening's sill and angled toward the room's interior. The masonry frame and sloped sill remain today.

The adobe platform on the floor was described in the original excavation report as "altar-like." Positioned in the northwest corner of the room, it was constructed as a raised section (4.9 by 1.3 feet) of the floor over a prepared foundation. Two shallow pits located at the north end

MAJOR ASTRONOMICAL ALIGNMENTS
AT SALMON RUINS

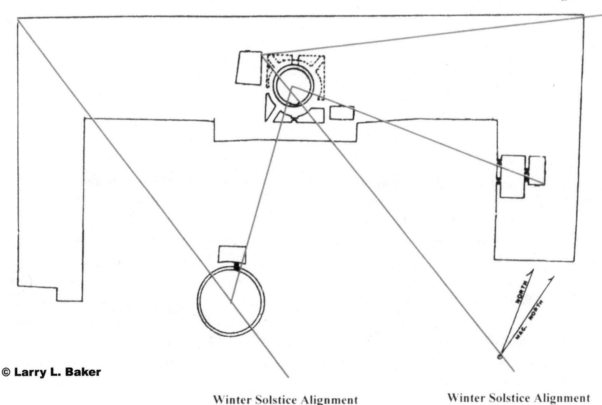

Figure 6.2. A first-story floor plan of Salmon Pueblo identifying a series of astronomical observation alignments used for the site's constructional "blueprint." © Salmon Ruins Museum.

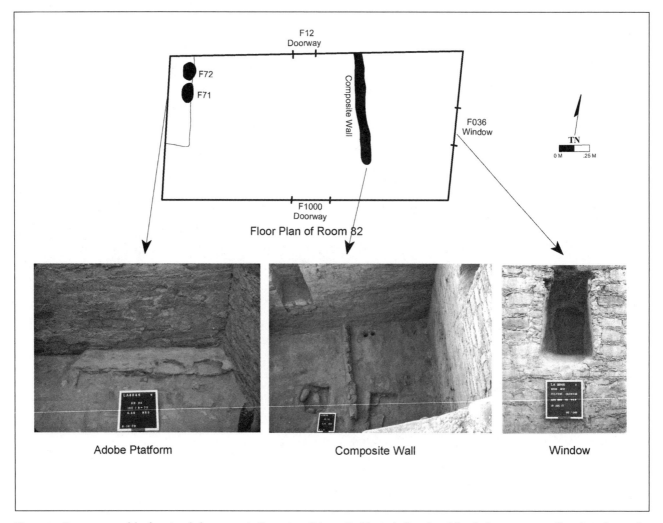

F12
Doorway

F72
F71

Composite Wall

F036
Window

TN
0 M   .25 M

F1000
Doorway

Floor Plan of Room 82

Adobe Ptatform

Composite Wall

Window

Figure 6.3. Components of the functional observatory in Room 82 at Salmon Pueblo, including the adobe platform, narrow wall, and window in the east wall. © Salmon Ruins Museum.

of the feature originally contained charcoal. The narrow divider wall was constructed of coursed-sandstone masonry with upright wooden poles spaced at regular intervals. Located approximately one-third of the room's length from the east wall, the wall was low at the time of excavation and likely never extended to the ceiling.

In 2008, Brooks Marshall reconstructed the features of the room that served as components of the functional observatory, using the detailed excavation records curated at the Salmon Ruins Museum. We positioned a plywood box at the same level as the adobe platform on the room's floor and two cobbles on its north end to simulate the adobe pits. We used a shade to simulate the divider wall on the floor.

In the early morning of the summer solstice (June 21), as well as for three days before and three days after, the sun shines through the window, and its light moves down the wall, striking the northernmost feature (a cobble) on the replica of the adobe platform (fig. 6.4). The sun illuminates this portion of the platform for approximately fifteen minutes before its light slowly fades from the feature, disappearing as it strikes the floor, with the shade-as-divider-wall in place. At no other point during the year does the sun shine on the "altar-like" feature. Thus, we are convinced that the integrated features in Room 82 serve as an observation station for designating an important point in time—the longest day of the year.

Figure 6.4. Sun striking the adobe platform replica in Room 82 at Salmon Pueblo on June 21, 2010. © Salmon Ruins Museum, courtesy of Larry L. Baker, photographer.

The platform feature in Room 82 also served to monitor lunar movements. Marshall and I observed the moon at both the summer and winter solstices from inside Room 82. Given sufficient illumination during full phase, moonlight will strike both pits in the platform at consistent times over the roughly nine years of the lunar cycle. Moonlight shines on an open area of the platform adjacent to the pits during the period when the major lunar standstill—when the moon appears stationary on the horizon—is at its maximum, or northernmost, position. When the moon is not bright enough to illuminate the feature, a sky watcher positioned at the very end of the platform could nevertheless observe the cycles of the moon by looking through the window in the east wall.

The sophisticated astronomical knowledge of the Chacoan builders is demonstrated by the special features built into Room 82, as well as the broader relationship between the architectural design and floor plan of Salmon Pueblo and its builders' astute astronomical observations. Pueblo people carried this knowledge with them into the historic period, and, based on current ethnographic data, they continue to use astronomy to plan calendrical and ritual events.

Archaeologists and other researchers interested in archaeoastronomy have also studied several structures at Aztec Ruins. These include Aztec's West Ruin, the great kiva at Aztec West, and the Hubbard Tri-Wall (Hubbard Mound), just north of Aztec West. The alignments between the summer solstice sunrise (northeast) and winter solstice sunset (southwest) and, similarly, the winter solstice sunrise (southeast) and summer solstice sunset (northwest) form solar azimuths that were noted by ancient Chacoan astronomers. Aztec's West Ruin, the largest Chacoan structure outside of Chaco Canyon, is aligned to a solar azimuth: its principal, or back, wall is oriented along the arc of the solstice summer sunrise and the winter solstice sunset.

The main room of Aztec's great kiva is surrounded by a northern antechamber and fifteen peripheral chambers. Each of the peripheral chambers contains an interior and exterior doorway, as interpreted by Earl Morris in his reconstruction of the kiva (see chapter 5). These doorways are positioned to provide an observer with a view from outside of a peripheral chamber through the main room and through the doorways of the peripheral chamber on the opposite side of the kiva. Some archaeologists have argued that the positioning of the doorways facilitates astronomical observations related to solar and lunar events.

Four peripheral chambers and their respective doorways (two in each chamber) provide a mechanism for precise observations of sunrise and sunset during both the summer and winter solstices (fig. 6.5). The summer solstice sunrise shines through the doorway of a peripheral chamber on the northeast side of the building and can be viewed through the doorway of the opposite peripheral chamber on the southwest side of the kiva. The winter solstice sunset can be viewed through the same doorways by looking from northeast to southwest. At present, views of the winter solstice sunrise and summer solstice sunset through the great kiva are obstructed by one of the reconstructed roof support columns, which is wider than the original, but originally, the winter solstice sunrise shone through peripheral doorways on the southeast side of the structure and was viewed through the opposite doorways on the northwest side of the building. The summer solstice sunset would have been observed from the opposite direction through these same doorways.

From within the great kiva, through the doors of specific peripheral chambers, the full moon can be observed to rise in different locations as it moves from the northernmost to the southernmost positions of its cycle. Figure 6.5 shows the various full-moon alignments as recorded from 2004 through 2005. Of particular interest is the full-moon observation on June 21, which shows an alignment from the southern doorway and across the central firebox to the altar in the center of the kiva's antechamber on the north side of the building. Observations of the moon through the respective doorways of four of the peripheral chambers track from north to south and back again during the moon's 18.6-year cycle. The calendrical nature of these observations seems clear. The moon's orbit of Earth oscillates, gradually causing the moon to rise at different points on the horizon over the years. The entire cycle of the moon from north to south and back to north again takes 18.6 years. At each end of this swing, the moon appears to pause for about two years, rising at the same point on the horizon before beginning to move back toward the opposite end of the swing. The length of this lunar-standstill cycle certainly suggests that these lunar observations were less important for yearly agricultural activities and more connected to a longer-term ceremonial cycle.

The Hubbard Tri-Wall structure provides an interesting insight into potential changes in ceremonialism and cosmology in the latter occupational periods of the prehistoric Pueblo people of the area. Aztec became a northern seat of power after 1120, and the tri-wall structures there, including the Hubbard Site, may shed light on the mysteries institutionalized in sacred architecture at the end of the Chacoan period.

The Hubbard Tri-Wall was excavated in 1953 (fig. 6.6). Earlier structures were found below the tri-wall's architecture; however, the tri-wall architecture likely dates after 1130. The triple-walled structure is massive, consisting of three concentric walls with two outer "rings" subdivided into small architectural units by partitions. The inner ring contains eight rooms, and the outer ring is subdivided into fourteen rooms, if the entryway space is included. The subdivisions thus form twenty-two rooms, not including the central circular space, which is a kiva. The concentric walls are more massive than the partitions and built of continuous core-veneer masonry. The partitions are also made of core-veneer masonry and abut the concentric walls.

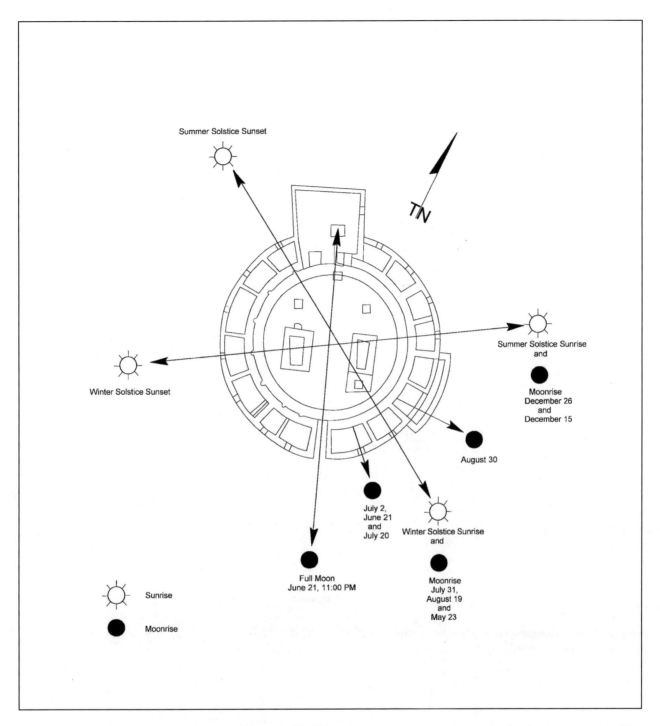

Figure 6.5. The great kiva at Aztec Ruins National Monument, noting alignments for both summer and winter solstices as well as positions of the full-moon alignments. Adapted from Gene Wheaton, "The Astronomy of Chaco Style Great Kivas" (MA thesis, University of Colorado Boulder, 2006).

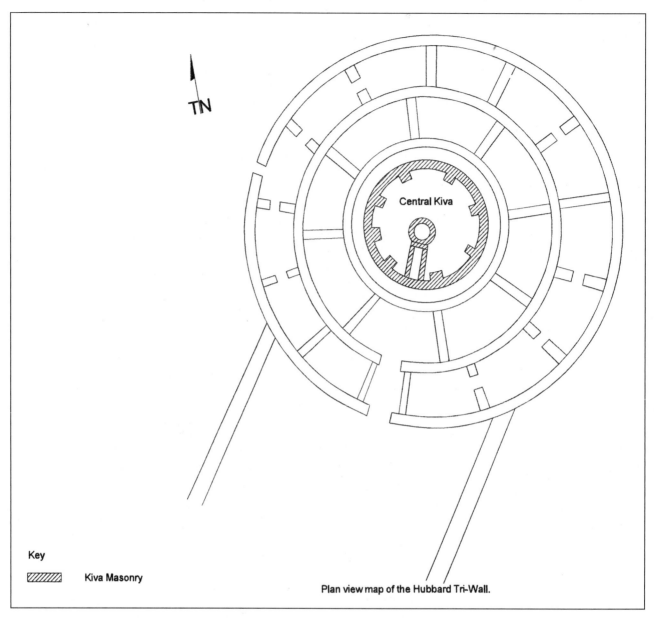

Figure 6.6. A map of the Hubbard Tri-Wall structure at Aztec Ruins National Monument. Adapted from R. Gwinn Vivian, "The Hubbard Site and other Tri-Wall Structures," *National Park Service Archeological Research Series* No. 5, 1959.

In a recent study of Aztec Ruins, Allan Mac-Gillivray III has suggested that the Hubbard Tri-Wall was a calendric site used to calculate the cycles of Venus. This suggestion is speculative and supported by little evidence. However, if MacGillivray is correct about ancient Puebloan observation of Venus's cycle, this might indicate that new, esoteric ritual knowledge was introduced to the Aztec community relatively late in the Puebloan sequence

(after 1130). Perhaps along these lines, Steve Lekson has suggested in his *Chaco Meridian* book that Aztec was a late post-Chacoan seat of power and that tri-wall structures were symbolic of this power—a new sheriff in town?

Nowhere are astronomical, and specifically lunar, observations more spectacular than at Chimney Rock, Colorado, at the very eastern margin of the Middle San Juan region. High above the valley of the Piedra River,

Figure 6.7. An aerial view of the Chacoan great house at Chimney Rock. Note the twin spires east of the great house, through which the moon rises at the major lunar standstill. Courtesy of the Chimney Rock Interpretive Association.

two bedrock spires (chimneys) dominate the landscape. The moon rises—perfectly framed—between these natural features during the major lunar standstill, a significant period in its cycle when it appears to hover in position over the horizon (see color plate 12).

By the eleventh century, if not sooner, inhabitants of the region had observed the moon rising between the spires at roughly eighteen-year intervals. The inhabitants of Chaco Canyon also became aware of this dramatic event. They were already sophisticated astronomers and subsequently constructed a great house at Chimney Rock. Based on tree-ring dates, we know that a large isolated kiva was initially built in 1076, a major-lunar-standstill date, and were proceeding with construction of a Chacoan-style great house by 1093, during another major-lunar-standstill event.

Due to its topographic position, the building would have been built at incredible cost in terms of labor and materials. Nevertheless, this classic Chacoan outlier would have afforded its builders a direct view of the moon rising between the twin spires of Chimney Rock. The Chacoan kiva and great house at Chimney Rock, in conjunction with this cyclic event, provide definitive proof that lunar standstills were incorporated into Chacoan astronomy and, by extension, into cosmology (fig. 6.7).

In summary, work by archaeologists, astronomers, and ethnographers in the field of archaeoastronomy has gone far beyond the mere examination and description of artifacts and architecture left behind by Pueblo peoples. Such studies have identified the celestial observations made by ancient peoples to mark time and, in a manner of speaking, to look into the future to predict events. In the Middle San Juan, architecture was closely tied to astronomy as well as ritual. The investment of time and labor by the inhabitants of Chaco Canyon and affiliated outlying communities was a testimony to the influence that astronomy and its associated esoteric knowledge had in guiding their amazing society.

In 2008, I had a momentary glimpse of the ritual power of astronomy when I witnessed the sun illuminate the altar feature in Room 82 at Salmon. This experience gave me goose bumps! Additional study will help us further understand the complicated relationship between architecture, astronomy, and cosmology in the Middle San Juan and across the ancient Southwest.

Larry L. Baker

Putting Meat on the Puebloan Table

Kathy Roler Durand and Ethan Ortega

In prehistoric times, a Pueblo hunter would have spent a lifetime perfecting his technique. From a young age, a boy learned the nuances of tracking deer and other large game animals. For smaller game, he learned how to construct a snare from cordage and how to find the best places for setting a trap—to maximize his chances of success. He spent winter nights around the fire, preparing arrowheads and spearpoints for the coming year, carefully hafting them to wooden shafts, and listening to stories of hunting adventures from long ago. As he matured into a young man, his hunting meant feast or famine for his growing family, providing strong incentive to hone his skills. Throughout his lifetime, a hunter would leave thousands of bones in trash heaps, a tribute to his hunting prowess. Indeed, one hunter, together with his kinfolk and descendants, could deposit tens of thousands of bones in trash heaps scattered across his territory.

Why would prehistoric hunters devote so much time to hunting when they had ready access to a variety of plant foods? Around the world, people of many cultures love meat, and their bodies cannot function well without the iron, fat, and vitamin B12 found in it. Although some iron can be obtained from plants, our bodies absorb iron from animal sources much more readily than from plant sources. Vitamin B12 is primarily available from meat or through modern supplements. So "What's for dinner?" was an important question for the health and well-being of prehistoric communities. In the days before we could pick up a roast at the corner grocery store, hunting was not a hobby, it was a crucial responsibility.

The people of the Middle San Juan region did not have the advantage of wild sheep or goats roaming the Southwest, ready to enter a domesticated relationship with the Pueblo people. That came a few centuries later, when the Spaniards introduced these now-familiar animals. Instead, when people across the Southwest wanted meat, they had to hunt or trap it. The two exceptions to this rule were dogs and turkeys. In historic times, the inhabitants of most pueblos raised dogs as pets or hunting companions, but they were rarely eaten. Wild turkeys were hunted early on, but in later prehistory domestic turkeys were raised in increasingly large numbers at many sites across the northern Southwest. We see evidence of them in the form of turkey pens, hundreds of eggshell fragments, juvenile bones, and even healed leg and wing bones, demonstrating that people cared for turkeys as the birds recovered from injuries. Bone-chemistry studies reveal that the turkeys in the later San Juan period (1190–1280 CE) ate about the same amount of corn as the humans who were raising them. It appears that the trade-off of feeding much of their corn to turkeys became worth the cost to the Middle San Juan inhabitants as deer declined in number, likely from overhunting, which has been documented in other regions across the Southwest.

What is the archaeologist's role in this story? Well, nearly a thousand years later we collect the remains of many hunting trips, including bones, and painstakingly reconstruct a hunter's success on the laboratory table (fig. 7.1). To the trained observer, the bones contain a wealth of information about the species hunted and the butchery techniques used to process carcasses, and sometimes even details about the season in which kills were made.

Around the world, people have preferred large game such as deer over small game such as cottontails

Figure 7.1. Zooarchaeologists identify fragmentary animal bones in a slow, meticulous process similar to working on a jigsaw puzzle. Courtesy of Ethan Ortega, photographer.

or jackrabbits, in part due to the substantially better return rate for large game. Our hunter would have had to capture more than fifty cottontail rabbits to provide as much meat as a single deer could bring. The difference would be even greater for larger species such as bighorn sheep or elk. Beyond the simple mathematics of larger size, many people prefer the taste of larger game animals. For the hunter, however, the biggest incentive may have been the prestige associated with returning to camp bearing such a large quantity of life-sustaining meat. Not only could he provide his own family with food, but he would have had extra meat to share with other members of his group. And cross-cultural studies of modern groups that rely on wild plants and animals for all or part of their diets reveal that successful hunters produce more offspring. Their advantage varies, but as many as 25 percent of the children born in these groups have the same father—who just happens to be the group's most

successful hunter. Clearly, the benefits of hunting success were myriad.

In the prehistoric Southwest, four primary species of large game were available for the hunt—deer, pronghorn (sometimes mistakenly called antelope), bighorn sheep, and elk. Each of these species had its own set of physical strengths and weaknesses, a unique response to danger, and particular habitat preferences. A successful hunter needed a thorough understanding of these traits for each species. Hunters in some areas specialized in a single species, such as pronghorn in the Great Basin or bison in the northern plains, likely because of the abundance in the region or the susceptibility to communal hunting practices.

In general, bighorn sheep and pronghorn can be hunted communally with nets or traps, while deer are more often obtained singly. Pronghorn tend to aggregate in open plains and in larger numbers than deer, and

Kathy Roler Durand and Ethan Ortega

they are known for their incredible speed and curiosity. This curiosity has led modern hunters to use tricks such as hanging brightly colored cloth to flap in the breeze in order to lure pronghorn into range. Bighorn sheep normally inhabit rocky terrains and are known for their agility and keen eyesight. The tendency of both species to congregate in large groups and flee rapidly from danger makes them ideal for net or trap hunting, in which herds are spooked and driven into premade enclosures, at which point the animals that are caught in the trap are clubbed to death. Both traps and clubs have been recovered at prehistoric sites in the western United States.

While the differences among deer may be more subtle, mule deer and white-tailed deer prefer different habitats and consequently have different responses to perceived dangers, such as an approaching hunter. Mule deer, in their more open habitat, will flee from danger, but white-tailed deer often attempt to hide in thick vegetation, allowing danger to bypass them. Mule deer migrate between summer and winter habitats along regular routes, and this behavior helps hunters predict their whereabouts during certain times of the year. White-tailed deer typically spend their lives within one small area and do not migrate seasonally. Deer of both varieties can be hunted in many different ways, including singly or as a group, although older bucks are more difficult to hunt successfully than are females or juveniles.

A common obstacle we face in reconstructing the types of game brought home by Pueblo hunters is something archaeologists call the "schlepp effect." Although pronghorn can be carried on the shoulders and brought many miles back to camp, other species of large game are too heavy to carry and must be butchered at the kill site. Simply put, with these species, only meat and the bones that had the fleshiest portions were lugged back to camp—the head, feet, and other heavy elements with little meat were left at the kill site. This combination of the schlepp effect and the size difference between large and small game means that even though an assemblage may contain lots of bones from small game such as cottontails and just a few bones from large game such as deer, most of the meat in the people's diet may still have been deer. More than simply counting the bones of each species left in a trash heap, we have to consider the amount of meat that those bones represent in order to figure out how much large game and small game actually contributed to people's diets.

Small game, such as the ubiquitous rabbit, also varies from species to species in terms of the amount of meat available per animal, preferred habitats, and behavior. Based on evidence from prehistoric and modern hunting, we can infer that small-game animals were hunted mostly when deer and other large game were scarce. Nevertheless, jackrabbits and cottontails were an important component of the diet in the Middle San Juan. Although jackrabbits and cottontails are similar species in terms of appearance and size, they have very different responses to the same environmental stimuli, which makes jackrabbits easier to hunt communally and obtain in greater numbers than cottontails. For example, when faced with danger, jackrabbits will flee, making them susceptible to net hunting by groups of humans, as was documented by the earliest chroniclers to visit the Southwest. Cottontails, by contrast, will attempt to hide in burrows or brush when faced with danger. Thus, they are not easily caught in large numbers with nets. Rabbits of all types also can be successfully hunted with throwing sticks. These are still used by Pueblo people today, and prehistoric examples are on display at the visitor center at Aztec Ruins National Monument.

It is possible that rodents were part of the Ancestral Pueblo diet, as prairie dogs were at sites in the Great Basin to the northwest. However, the rarity of cut marks and burning on rodent bones suggests that most died of natural causes, not as a result of human activity. Fish bones are also rare at sites in the Middle San Juan region, suggesting that fish were not an important component of the prehistoric diet. Only a few of the Middle San Juan sites have produced any fish bones, despite the fact that these communities were located along two of the region's three permanent rivers. Perhaps there was a cultural taboo against eating this plentiful source of protein, or a lack of fishing technology in the region.

Finally, reproductive differences between large- and small-bodied species also influence their availability for hunting. Smaller-bodied species tend to reproduce more quickly, while larger species are slower to produce the same number of offspring. Over time, as our hunter and

Figure 7.2. Room 128 was one of the turkey pens at Salmon Pueblo. This unusually long room was located on the southeast corner of the structure and contained turkey bones, eggshells, and a turkey pit-pen. © Salmon Ruins Museum.

his kin were actively taking animals in the Middle San Juan region, the smaller species such as rabbits were able to recover from the effects of hunting more quickly than were the large-bodied animals such as deer or elk. A drop in the frequency of large species over time has been documented for a number of regions across the west, including the Middle San Juan.

Given such variables as animal behavior and reproduction, as well as differences in hunting methods for each species, we see that "What's for dinner?" was not a simple question at all. Along with other researchers, we have studied animal bones from three different sites or communities in the Middle San Juan region: the Tommy Site, the Aztec community, and Salmon Pueblo (which represents our largest sample). For the time period considered in this volume, we see a clear drop in the amount of large game hunted—from nearly three-fourths of the

bones identified at the Aztec community's North Mesa sites in the Chacoan period to less than a one-fourth of the bones at Aztec West after 1200. At the same time, turkey remains increase from a handful in the Chacoan period at the Aztec community to nearly a third of the bones in the San Juan period (1125–1280) at Salmon Pueblo. Several rooms (including a very long Room 128) at Salmon Pueblo during this period were converted into turkey pens (fig. 7.2). Because turkeys would have required extra work to raise, we assume this decrease in the bones of large game reflects its absence in the region. Even if the human population in a region remains the same, large-game animals can be overhunted and decrease in number, and this pattern has been found prehistorically from southern Arizona to the Mimbres region of southwest New Mexico and as far north as southern Colorado. To compensate for the decrease in

Kathy Roler Durand and Ethan Ortega

Plate 1. An aerial view of Salmon Pueblo along the San Juan River, 1983. © Adriel Heisey, photographer.

Plate 2. An aerial view of Aztec West, Aztec Ruins National Monument, 1983. The Hubbard Tri-Wall structure is visible in the lower right corner of the photo. © Adriel Heisey, photographer.

Plate 3. An aerial view of the sprawling ancient Pueblo community now known as the Holmes Group, on the eastern edge of La Plata Valley, 2007. © Adriel Heisey, photographer.

Plate 4. A view of the interior of the reconstructed Great Kiva at Aztec Ruins National Monument, 2016. The National Park Service completed work on the structure in 1934 with a Works Progress Administration crew supervised by Earl Morris. Courtesy of Lori Reed, photographer.

Plate 5. A view of Mount Taylor, or Kaweshtiima in the Acoma Keres language, from McCartys Village at Acoma Pueblo, New Mexico. Courtesy of Theresa Pasqual, photographer.

Plate 6. A photograph of modern wild turkeys. Turkeys were an important part of the Ancestral Pueblo diet and a source of feathers for blankets and various artifacts. Courtesy of Jack Ellis, photographer.

(*left*) Plate 7. Three-dimensional models showing central Mesa Verde region villages. Courtesy of the Crow Canyon Archaeological Center, Dennis Holloway, modeler, and Adriel Heisey, photographer.

(*below*) Plate 8. Pottery sherds from the collections at Aztec Ruins National Monument. Note the differences in colors and painted designs. All of the redware pottery shown here is White Mountain Red Ware, made far to the south near Zuni, New Mexico, and Show Low, Arizona. The black piece in the top right corner is part of a Mogollon Brown Ware bowl, also made in east-central Arizona. The whiteware piece in the top left corner has the signature Chacoan hatched design, but many of the other black-on-white pieces here represent post-Chaco-era styles. The two sherds with finger-indented coils are from grayware cooking pots. Courtesy of the Aztec Ruins National Monument, Lori Reed, photographer.

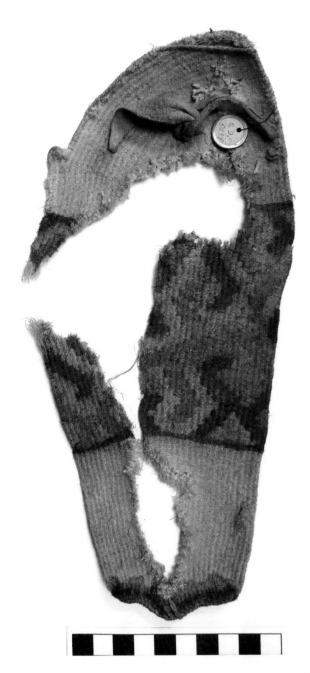

Plate 9. A yucca twined sandal with red and brown design, jogged toe, and hide double toe loops, from the West Ruin of Aztec, second story, Room 122, early occupation. Courtesy of the Division of Anthropology, American Museum of Natural History (AMNH 29.0/5289), Laurie Webster, photographer.

Plate 10. Cotton diamond-twill fabric with red, brown, and natural white banded design, from the West Ruin of Aztec, Room 189, early occupation. Courtesy of the Aztec Ruins National Monument (AZRU 1773), Laurie Webster, photographer.

Plate 11. Cotton 2/1 twill fabric with red, brown, and natural white banded design, from the West Ruin of Aztec, Room 193, undetermined occupation. Courtesy of the Aztec Ruins National Monument (AZRU 2724), Laurie Webster, photographer.

Plate 12. The rise of the full moon on the lunar standstill between the pillars at Chimney Rock National Monument, Colorado. Courtesy of G. B. Cornucopia, photographer.

Plate 13. The Great House at Aztec West. Courtesy of the National Park Service, Cheryl Paddock, photographer.

Plate 14. The west facade of the Great House at Aztec West, featuring decorative banding in the exterior masonry, with green stone and thin sandstone courses. Courtesy of the National Park Service, Gary Brown, photographer.

Plate 15. One of Timothy O'Sullivan's photographs of Salmon Pueblo, 1874, during the Wheeler Survey. The photographer himself is posed in the room along with a helper, another glass-plate camera, a scale, and his coat, which is hung on a peg in the wall. Beyond the historic interest of the photograph, readers will note the beautiful Chacoan masonry (stone) veneer pattern shown in the image. Courtesy of Timothy O'Sullivan, photographer.

Plate 16. A reconstruction of Salmon Pueblo, as it might have appeared in 1100 CE. The view is from the west wing of the pueblo, looking east toward the San Juan River (not visible) and distant terrace across the river. Readers will note the massive construction of the Salmon building and the abundant corn depicted growing in the river's floodplain. © Salmon Ruins Museum, created by Doug Gann, Archaeology Southwest, Salmon Project, 2006.

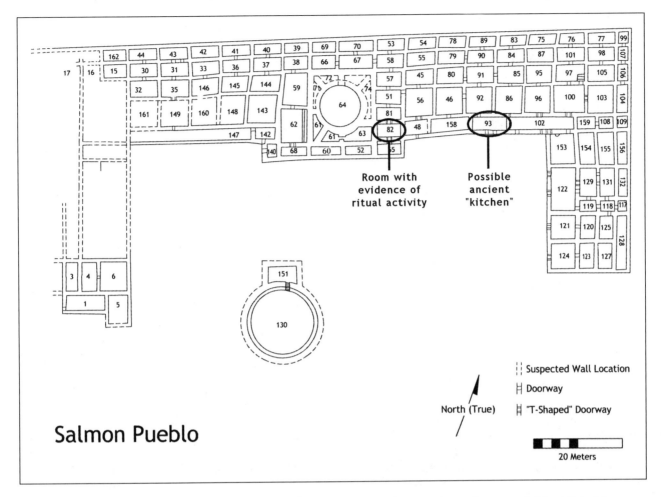

Figure 7.3. A map of Salmon Pueblo (during the Chacoan period) showing locations of rooms with special activities. © Salmon Ruins Museum.

large game, people in many communities began to raise turkeys.

In addition to changes through time, we can document different activities that occurred at the same site during the same time period. An example comes from two rooms at Salmon Pueblo that were used during the Chacoan period. One of these, Room 93, faces the plaza in the eastern half of the main roomblock. The bones from this room reveal that people actively prepared food here. The animals processed in this room were nearly all rabbits and large game, including cottontails, jackrabbits, and deer. Most of the deer elements were meat-bearing limb bones. Almost all of the bones had been broken into pieces and burned, indicating that people extracted the fat and protein-rich marrow. The presence of several hearths and milling bins for processing corn also supports the interpretation of this room as an ancient kitchen (fig. 7.3).

Room 82, by contrast, contained bones that were very different from those we found in Room 93. This room was adjacent to the pueblo's Tower Kiva and would not have been easily accessible. We found many more species in Room 82, despite the fact that both rooms contained about the same number of bones. In addition to deer and rabbit bones, which were also present in Room 93, Room 82 had bones from two other species that likely were eaten—pronghorns and turkeys—as well as bones from several animals that likely were not part of the diet, including coyotes, bobcats, small and medium-sized songbirds, lizards, and snakes. Some of these latter species are important components of religious ceremonies among Pueblo people, who still today use their feathers and pelts as part of costumes, prayer sticks, and other offerings. Elements of Room 82's carnivores included paw and skull bones, which are typically

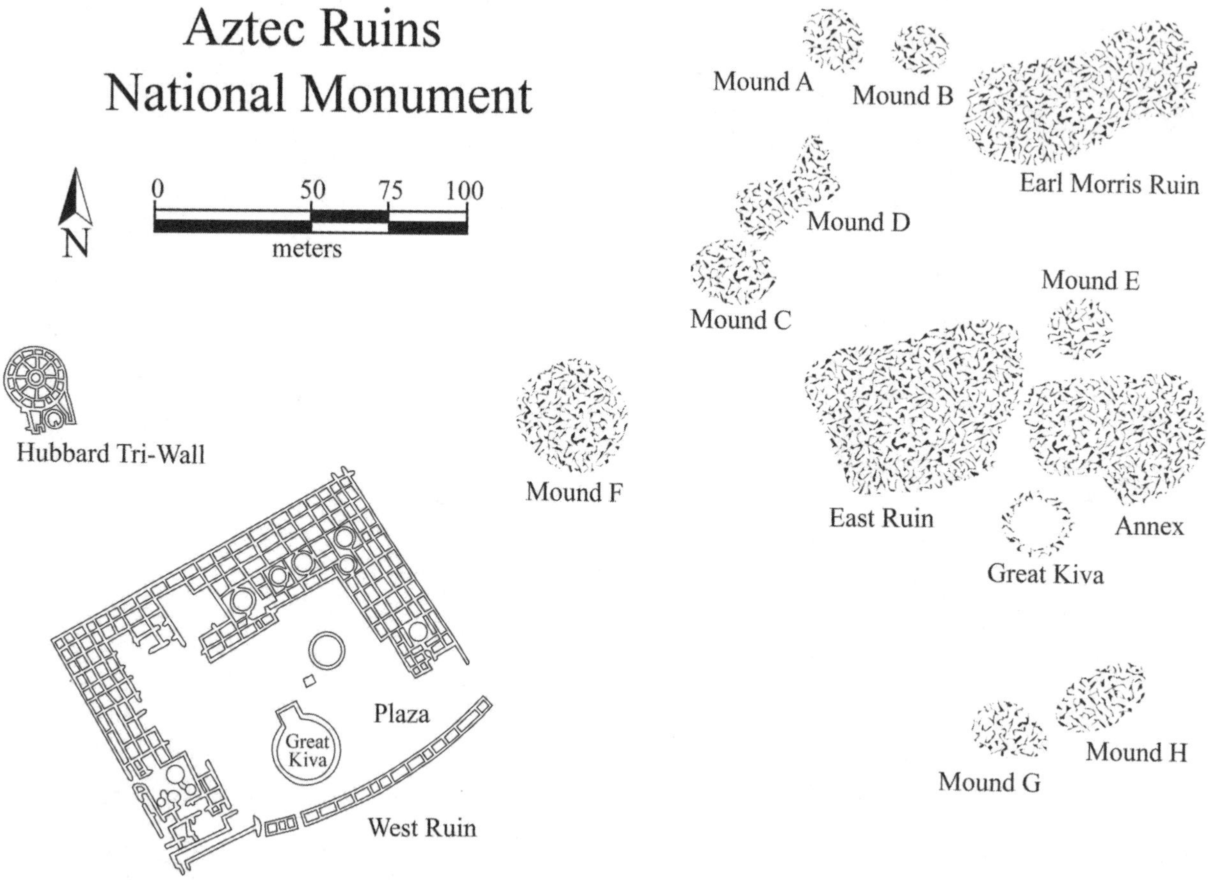

Aztec Ruins
National Monument

Figure 7.4. The location of Mound E, Aztec Ruins National Monument. The mound lies just northeast of Aztec's East Ruin. Courtesy of the National Park Service.

left with the skin when animal pelts are prepared. Most of the large-game bones in this room were skull fragments, which are used for many different ceremonies and often coated or filled with a special cornmeal.

The pattern we discovered in the bones fits with Larry Baker's evidence that Room 82 was used as an astronomical observatory to mark the summer solstice and lunar-standstill events (see chapter 6). The presence of species with known religious importance, the evidence of the room's use as an observatory, its location adjacent to Salmon Pueblo's Tower Kiva, and the low level of accessibility to the room all suggest it was a location for religious activity and a storage room for materials used in the ceremonies held in the adjacent kiva. Our hunter and his kin would have brought some of the fruits of his labors to both Rooms 82 and 93, but they would have been used for different purposes in each.

We found another intriguing pattern of bones at Mound E in the Aztec community (fig. 7.4). This mound,

according to archaeologist Gary Brown, appears to have been a specialized midden with a large amount of ash in the fill. Based on the type of pottery found there, we know that the deposit is from the post-Chacoan period, and it was unique in terms of its nature and location just to the north of Aztec's eastern great house. We find the bones from Mound E especially interesting because this deposit dates from the later period of regional occupation, when large-game animals were apparently becoming scarce, and yet nearly 60 percent of bones excavated at this midden were from large game (representing at least two bighorn sheep and likely one deer). The mound also contained a higher percentage of turkey remains than found elsewhere in the Aztec community, as well as some of the only fish remains identified at Aztec to date, representing at least two species—squawfish and sucker.

Although archaeologists excavated only a small test unit, the nature of the deposit (including the very ashy sediments) and its location just behind and downwind

Kathy Roler Durand and Ethan Ortega

Figure 7.5. A view of the scarlet macaw discovered under the door sill between Rooms 97 and 100 at Salmon Pueblo. © Salmon Ruins Museum.

of the great house suggest that the mound might contain a unique assemblage—possibly related to feasting at the great house—like those found at Mississippian sites such as Cahokia and Moundville. The high numbers of large animals and turkeys represented by the Mound E bones differ from the patterns found in the rest of the community and, at the least, show that some kind of distinctive activity was occurring in this area.

We know of one other distinctive aspect of the animal bones found in the Middle San Juan, but in this case it has nothing to do with diet. As we mentioned in relation to Room 82 at Salmon Pueblo, people trapped and hunted some species (such as carnivores and small colorful birds) that they had no intention of eating. Ancestral and modern Pueblo groups have used many parts of certain animals, such as feathers, pelts, paws, claws, and skulls, for costumes and ceremonial offerings as part of their religion. While most of these species could be obtained from the local environs around their

communities, occasionally they needed a species that was not available locally. Archaeologists have found the skeletons of scarlet macaws at Chacoan sites across the northern Southwest and at sites in other regions beyond the Chacoan world. Macaws have also been found in Chaco Canyon: the remains of thirty-one macaws were recovered in the eastern half of the great house of Pueblo Bonito, and an additional five were found at Pueblo del Arroyo, just across the Chaco Wash from Pueblo Bonito.

Archaeologists recovered the remains of two scarlet macaws at Aztec and the remains of nine more at Salmon Pueblo, most of the scarlet variety and at least one even rarer military macaw (fig. 7.5). Both species have brilliant plumage, awash in reds, blues, and golds not readily obtained in nature. For the people of the Middle San Juan to have acquired these colorful treasures, one or more individuals had to traverse the hundreds of miles to their habitats in what is now central and southern Mexico. While later prehistory saw the rise of Paquimé,

Figure 7.6. While many turkeys were eaten and their bones were then tossed into trash middens, some received formal burials at sites across the Southwest. © Salmon Ruins Museum.

Figure 7.7. Other artifacts, for example, lithic tools, were often found adjacent to turkey burials. © Salmon Ruins Museum.

a trading center in northern Mexico that was well stocked with macaws, this center was not in existence until after the Chacoan period. A further difficulty of the trade in macaws was the nature of the birds themselves. Far from docile and easygoing, these large, sometimes trying birds have powerful beaks to back up their squawks of protest for any less-than-friendly treatment they may receive. It is not surprising that most macaw skeletons in the prehistoric Southwest hover around one year in age, which maximized plumage formation but minimized the time required to cope with a mature, cantankerous bird.

Macaws often were interred whole, thus their preservation is excellent. Interestingly, some turkeys were interred in a similar manner, although most turkey bones were disposed of in the trash heaps along with the other remains of daily meals. Turkey burials have been found at Salmon Pueblo; Galaz Ruin in the Mimbres region; Grasshopper Pueblo in east-central Arizona; a site near Taos, New Mexico; and several sites in Chaco Canyon and the Mesa Verde region (figs. 7.6 and 7.7). At several of these sites, people buried turkeys in rooms that also contained human and macaw burials.

Kathy Roler Durand and Ethan Ortega

Along with macaw feathers, Ancestral Pueblo people incorporated turkey feathers into ritual objects, such as prayer sticks, and wove feathers into robes or blankets (see chapter 8). Laurie Webster has studied the perishable artifacts from several Chacoan great houses, including Salmon Pueblo, and notes that of the individuals buried at Salmon with perishable materials surviving to the present day, nearly half were buried with either a fur or feather blanket. Turkey-feather blankets were nearly always present among the well-preserved burials found at Aztec. Feather ornaments, cordage, and socks have also been identified. Thus, turkeys were multipurpose birds that came to comprise a large portion of the meat diet for the Middle San Juan's inhabitants after 1200 but were also used for ritual purposes throughout the region's occupation.

In the end, we should not be surprised that turkeys played so many different roles in the day-to-day lives of people in the Middle San Juan. These resourceful people made use of every available material to survive through times of hardship and to thrive in times of plenty. In our modern, compartmentalized world, few things traverse freely between our religious and practical lives. Yet the turkey may be the best symbol to help us remember how, nearly one thousand years ago, when offerings of thanks and gratitude were made to the spirits prior to every hunt and planting season, these ancient people survived difficult seasons in the Middle San Juan, until circumstances finally forced them to move away. When the Spanish first arrived in the Southwest, they noted the presence of huge flocks of turkeys at the pueblos along the Rio Grande, demonstrating that our hunter's descendants kept this pattern of resource use alive after their migration from the Middle San Juan to the Rio Grande. They successfully adapted to changes in the regional availability of large game by raising turkeys, which provided another source of protein for their sustenance and more meat for their tables.

Acknowledgments

We would like to thank Paul Reed and Gary Brown for inviting us to contribute to this volume. We are grateful to several individuals for reading and commenting on earlier drafts, including James Gore, Suzanne Balch-Lindsay, Kerriann Marden, Sue Strickler, and Betty Williamson. In addition to our own data, we used data gathered by Jack Bertram, Erin Enright, and Lee-Anna Schniebs to describe parts of the Aztec community and the Tommy Site, and we thank them for their careful analysis.

Ancient Puebloan Clothing from the Aztec and Salmon Great Houses

Laurie D. Webster

It is a warm spring day at Aztec Ruins National Monument on the outskirts of Aztec, New Mexico. Visitors in T-shirts, jeans, and sneakers cluster around an individual wearing a distinctive uniform: a short-sleeved gray shirt adorned with a gold shield-shaped badge, a name tag, and an arrowhead-shaped patch; olive green pants; a brown cordovan belt; oxford shoes; and a wide-brimmed straw hat with an embossed leather band. The visitors listen attentively as the individual shares a few introductory remarks, then leads a procession through the abandoned rooms of this once-great pueblo, into the open-air plaza, and down a short flight of stairs into the partially underground great kiva, where the group enters a subterranean realm, a site of ancient rituals.

Can you identify the person of authority in this group? Of course you can. Anyone who has visited a national park in the United States can immediately recognize the costume and insignia of a National Park Service ranger. This highly regulated uniform identifies the wearer as a person with specialized knowledge, while its badges and patches convey status, responsibility, and authority. Although this person possesses many social identities, the costume is intended to express just one, obscuring the rest behind a veil of uniformity.

Clothing—the most visible aspect of human ornamentation—is also a supreme marker of social identities. It can convey membership in social groups and also differentiate individuals from one another. It can communicate age, gender, social status, and economic role, as well as social, political, or religious affiliation. The correct interpretation of these clothing messages often requires access to in-group cultural knowledge. For example, only someone well versed in the hierarchy of

the Catholic Church can distinguish a cardinal, bishop, or monsignor by the color and suite of his vestments (sacred clothing). However, some assemblages, such as that worn by our park ranger, can be easily understood by perfect strangers.

Based on what we currently know about the clothing worn in the ancient North American Southwest, these same observations also held true for pre-Hispanic Southwesterners. Archaeologists have recovered thousands of textile fragments and a few complete garments from cliff dwellings and great houses in the Four Corners region of the Colorado Plateau, along with areas to the south and west. From the pioneering research of Southwestern textile scholar Kate Peck Kent, we know that during the period 1000–1300 CE, women wore some form of apron, men a breechcloth, and both made use of cotton blankets and turkey-feather robes for daily dress. Both sexes probably also wore yucca sandals and may have worn shoe-socks with animal-hair or turkey-feather pile. By the end of this period, if not before, a man would have donned some combination of a special shirt, tunic, sash, breechcloth, kilt, or painted or tie-dyed blanket for more formal occasions, such as a religious observance, and women would have begun wearing their cotton blankets as wraparound dresses, over one shoulder and under the other and secured around the waist with a sash. All of these styles are depicted in kiva mural paintings dating to the period 1350–1600, made by the descendants of these groups living in the Hopi area and the Rio Grande Valley, and many of these same garments are still worn in ceremonies by modern Pueblo people.

Kent based most of her interpretations about pre-Hispanic dress during the 1000–1300 period on assemblages from cliff dwellings in Arizona, southeastern Utah, and southwestern Colorado, not great-house communities in northwestern New Mexico. The principal excavators of these great houses—George Pepper and Neil Judd in Chaco Canyon, Earl Morris at Aztec West, and Cynthia Irwin-Williams at Salmon Pueblo—published relatively few of the textiles they found. Consequently, when I began my study of the textiles, baskets, and other perishable artifacts from Salmon, Aztec, and Chaco Canyon in the early 2000s, I knew relatively little about the clothing worn in these great-house communities. I was amazed to discover that excavations at Salmon had yielded more than seven hundred perishable artifacts, excavations at Pueblo Bonito nearly one thousand, and at Aztec roughly seventeen hundred. Although the vast majority of these artifacts are not articles of dress (the collections also contain a wide array of baskets, matting, cordage, wooden implements, and other organic objects), the textiles demonstrate that the inhabitants of these great houses wore the same general types of clothing as their neighbors to the north and west, but also that they used some distinctive articles not reported elsewhere.

What, then, is presently known about the clothing worn by the people of Salmon Pueblo and Aztec West? To answer this question, we must consider two time periods: the Chacoan period , when people wore clothing similar to that worn in Chaco Canyon, dating from 1090 or 1100 to roughly 1140, and a post-Chacoan period from about 1140 to 1280, when the clothing worn at Salmon and Aztec more closely resembled that worn at Mesa Verde to the north. Most of the surviving clothing from this latter period dates to the early to mid-1200s, with relatively little information available for the transitional time period between 1140 and 1200.

Researchers have convincingly argued that groups of Chacoan people migrated to Salmon and Aztec during and following the construction of these pueblos in the late 1000s and early 1100s. The textile evidence supports this migration scenario. Based on textiles recovered from the same early rooms at Aztec West where ceramics specialist Lori Reed identified large deposits of Chaco-made pottery (see chapter 9), we know that the clothing of these early occupants

Figure 8.1. The lower face of a yucca 2/2 twill-plaited sandal with a jogged toe and a raised zigzag design, West Ruin of Aztec, Room 115, probably Chacoan occupation. Courtesy of the Division of Anthropology, American Museum of Natural History (AMNH 29.0/8855), Laurie Webster, photographer.

included finely woven twined sandals, twill-plaited sandals, looped shoe-socks, and cotton fabrics made from plain and twill weaves. Although no definite examples of women's aprons or men's breechcloths have been identified, these articles were presumably worn, too. Because burial assemblages with preserved perishable artifacts are rare at Salmon and nonexistent at Aztec during the Chacoan period, we know little about how these early residents dressed their loved ones for burial. The one early burial with perishables from Salmon, identified by Irwin-Williams as that of an individual who may have belonged to a bow or other ceremonial society, included cotton cloth, a twined fur or feather

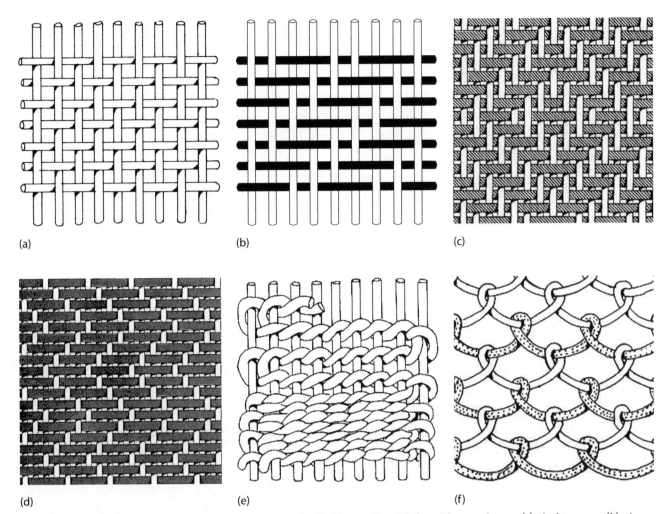

(a)

(b)

(c)

(d)

(e)

(f)

Figures 8.2a–8.2f. The most common weave structures used to make the fabrics and sandals from Salmon and Aztec: (a) 1/1 plain weave, (b) 2/2 twill weave, (c) diamond-twill weave, (d) reverse or herringbone-twill weave, (e) two-strand twining, and (f) simple looping. Structures 8.2a–d were used to make cotton cloth; 8.2b was used to make twill-plaited yucca sandals; 8.2e was used to make twined sandals and a feathered-yucca belt or headband; and 8.2f was used to make a feathered-yucca fabric and human-hair leggings. Adapted from Kate Peck Kent, *Prehistoric Textiles of the Southwest* (Santa Fe, NM: School of American Research, 1983), figs. 14c, 51a, 62, 90, 91.

blanket, and a bulrush, twill-plaited mat, as well as a bow, arrows, and a reed cylinder or quiver.

Yucca sandals outnumber all other articles of clothing in the early textile remains from Aztec and Salmon (fig. 8.1). Two styles were worn: twined and twill-plaited. Twined sandals became popular on the Colorado Plateau very early on, during the Basketmaker period (1–750), and were worn into the early 1200s. Densely woven of finely spun yucca yarns, many of these sandals have colored, tapestry-woven geometric designs on their upper surfaces, and most have raised geometric designs on their soles. This type of footwear enjoyed considerable use in Chaco Canyon into the early 1100s, based on evidence

from Pueblo Bonito, Chetro Ketl, and Pueblo del Arroyo. Chacoan versions dating to the early to mid-1000s have a rounded toe, but by the mid- to late 1100s, people were also wearing sandals with a distinctive toe jog along the outer edge. This jogged-toe style was also worn by the early occupants of Salmon and Aztec. At Aztec West, the popularity of twined sandals during the Chacoan period has been demonstrated by Morris's recovery of nearly fifty examples from a handful of rooms in the eastern and northern wings. Many of these early sandals have dark brown and occasionally red geometric designs, and some are woven in a slit-tapestry technique. At Aztec, they were attached to the foot by a pair of

Figure 8.3. A cotton diamond-twill tapestry fabric with a red, brown, and natural white serrated design, enclosing a rush bundle, from West Ruin of Aztec, probably Room 49, Chacoan occupation. Courtesy of the Division of Anthropology, American Museum of Natural History (AMNH 29.0/7319), Laurie Webster, photographer.

side-by-side toe loops, a heel strap, and a tie that ran between them. In many examples, the toe loops and heel straps were fashioned from hide strips. A twined sandal with side loops was also found at Salmon Pueblo.

These Chaco-era occupants of the pueblos also wore twill-plaited sandals that were made of yucca-leaf strips in a 2/2 (over two, under two) weave (fig. 8.2b). Prior to the construction of Salmon and Aztec, this style was fashionable in Chaco Canyon and several other areas of the Colorado Plateau. By the early 1100s, most of these twill-plaited sandals also had a jogged toe. The most elaborate twill-plaited sandals, recovered at Pueblo Bonito and Aztec West, have a raised zigzag design on the underside of the sole. During the late 1000s and early 1100s, the occupants of Aztec and Salmon fastened their twill-plaited sandals to their feet by means of a toe loop–heel strap arrangement, or less frequently, with side loops. The paired toe loops had the same side-by-side configuration as those used on the twined sandals. The loops, straps, and ties on these plaited sandals were typically made of yucca cordage, not hide.

During the Chaco interval, people also wore shoe-socks, a stockinglike form of footwear produced by a looping technique similar to crochet (fig. 8.2f). Chacoan examples are made from yucca cordage wrapped with either an animal-hair or turkey-feather pile, but the people of Salmon and Aztec seem to have used only the turkey-feather variety. At least one resident of Salmon Pueblo wore a shoe-sock with a looped turkey-feather upper and a plaited-yucca sandal sole (fig. 8.4).

The early inhabitants of these great houses also wore cotton textiles of plain and twill weaves. Because of their fragmentary nature, we do not know if these incomplete fabrics were parts of blankets or other garments. The people of Salmon are known to have used plain-weave and 2/1 (over two, under one) twill-weave cotton fabrics, but because all have been carbonized and are now black, we do not know if any had colored decoration. At Aztec West, Morris recovered a much wider range of cotton fabrics worked in plain weave, and diagonal, diamond, and herringbone twill (figs. 8.2a, 8.2b, 8.2c, 8.2d). Twill tapestry and diamond-twill tapestry fabrics were also found. Because unburned textiles were preserved there, we know that the plain-weave fabrics from the early occupation were natural white or colored solid red or dark brown, possibly with mineral pigments, and that the diagonal-twill fabrics often had white, red, or sometimes brown stripes in a horizontally banded layout. The twill-tapestry fabrics had a similar color palette worked in serrated or zigzag designs. The fanciest cotton textile from Aztec West, a diamond-twill tapestry fabric with a white, red, and brown zigzag pattern, is wrapped around a rush bundle that may have served as a badge of office for a religious or political leader (fig. 8.3).

We do not know whether all of these cotton fabrics were woven at Salmon and Aztec during the Chacoan period or if some were traded in from other communities. At least some were probably woven at Aztec, because Morris recovered two loom bars and a weaving batten from a ceremonial room behind the earliest Chacoan kiva. Based on the width of the loom bars and Morris's lack of reference to loom holes in the floor, the loom appears to have functioned as a wide backstrap loom, a simple horizontal loom with a strap that attaches to the weaver's back. Backstrap loom bars were also recovered from kiva and mortuary settings at Pueblo Bonito. At Salmon, four small wooden objects

that might have served as weaving battens were found in a ceremonial room adjacent to the earliest Chacoan kiva at the site.

Although archaeologists have found weaving tools and cotton fabrics at Aztec and Salmon, evidence for cotton cultivation there or in Chaco Canyon is surprisingly scarce. No cotton bolls or other plant parts and only a few cotton seeds have been found. It is possible that the early residents of Salmon and Aztec imported their cotton fiber and wove it into textiles themselves, or they may have imported most of their finished fabrics, especially the fancier weaves, which required specialized weaving knowledge to produce. At least some cotton textiles were imported into Chaco Canyon, because fine cotton lacelike fabrics almost certainly made in southern Arizona were found at Chetro Ketl. By the early 1100s, weaving centers in northeastern Arizona, such as Antelope House in Canyon del Muerto, were producing considerable quantities of cotton textiles, some of

Figure 8.4. A looped shoe-sock made of yucca cordage wrapped with turkey feathers, from West Ruin of Aztec, Room 193, probably post-Chacoan occupation. Courtesy of the Aztec Ruins National Monument (AZRU 1793), Laurie Webster, photographer.

Figure 8.5. A yucca looped fabric covered with feather-bearing cords, probably the remains of a feathered garment. Fine bright orange-red quills, probably from red-shafted northern flickers, are embedded in the cords, from West Ruin of Aztec, second story, Room 122, Chacoan occupation. Courtesy of the Division of Anthropology, American Museum of Natural History (AMNH 29.0/5285), Laurie Webster, photographer.

Figure 8.6. The corner of a cotton plain-weave textile with a pom-pom tassel and twine-stitch embroidery worked in a scroll-like design, from West Ruin of Aztec, Room 182, probably post-Chacoan occupation. Courtesy of the Aztec Ruins National Monument (AZRU 2723), Laurie Webster, photographer.

which could have found their way into these great-house communities.

We know relatively little about the specific articles of clothing worn in religious ceremonies at Salmon and Aztec during the late 1000s and early 1100s, but an assemblage from a religious storeroom at Aztec West provides a tantalizing glimpse of the ritual regalia worn during such events. It includes a twined yucca belt or headband originally covered with feathers from unidentified birds, a looped yucca fabric once covered with orange-red feathers (fig. 8.5), a cotton diagonal-twill textile with horizontal white and red stripes, a white cotton textile with small cotton pom-poms decorating the surface, an ornately patterned jogged-toe twined sandal with a red-and-brown interlocking scroll design worked in slit tapestry, and a cotton-twill tapestry fabric with a natural white, red, and brown serrated design and cinched at one end to make a possible bag. The feathered yucca garments have not been reported elsewhere in the Southwest and, as far as we know, are unique to Aztec. Their closest Southwestern analogs are three fragmentary bands threaded with red-shafted flicker feathers, possibly headdresses, found by Pepper at Pueblo Bonito.

Picture, if you will, a scenario like that described at the beginning of this chapter, but instead of a National Park Service ranger leading a group of visitors through

Figure 8.7. A child's moccasin with probable porcupine-quill decoration, from West Ruin of Aztec, Room 95, post-Chacoan occupation. Courtesy of the Division of Anthropology, American Museum of Natural History (AMNH 29.0/8965), Laurie Webster, photographer.

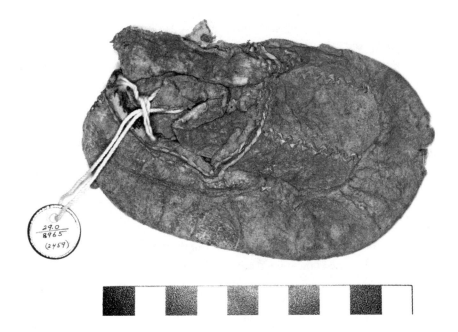

the plaza and into the great kiva, imagine an ancient procession of religious or political leaders leading local residents and members of neighboring communities. One individual wears a brilliant feather-covered belt or headband. Another wears a garment, perhaps a shirt, kilt, or breechcloth, smothered in orange-red feathers. One wears a white cotton garment adorned with small cotton pom-poms. Another wears a red-and-white-banded cotton blanket. One man carries a makeshift cotton bag decorated with red, brown, and white zigzags. Several people in the procession wear intricately decorated twined sandals on their feet, the raised designs on the soles leaving distinctive footprints in the soil. Others adorn their feet with finely woven twill-plaited sandals or turkey feather shoe-socks. This is just a hint of the fancy dress that would have been worn at Aztec West during the Chacoan period, because most ritual clothing has disappeared, leaving no archaeological trace.

Fast-forward fifty years to the time when the Chacoan system was in decline. From 1150 to 1280, the textile traditions of the later occupants of Salmon and Aztec underwent both losses and innovations as social ties shifted from Chaco Canyon to the Mesa Verde region in the north. Several styles of clothing worn during the initial occupation persisted into this later period, including undecorated plain-weave and banded twill-weave cotton blankets and twined and twill-plaited sandals. To our knowledge, however, the feather-embellished garments did not persist, nor did the fancy twill tapestry and diamond-twill tapestry fabrics. In their place, new types of clothing appeared, ones suggesting stronger social ties to the Mesa Verde region.

For example, while the later occupants of Aztec and Salmon continued to rely on twined turkey-feather blankets to keep them warm, the people of Aztec, and perhaps Salmon, appear to have decorated their fancier robes with geometric designs worked in dark and light turkey feathers. Perishables analyst Carolyn Osborne has identified similar blankets at Mesa Verde, noting that their makers drew designs on the warps with red pigment before wrapping them with light and dark feathers. I have seen a similarly decorated example from Grand Gulch in southeastern Utah. Although no intact examples of these decorated feather blankets survived at Aztec, fragments with areas of red pigment on the warps have been found, suggesting that they too were decorated in this manner. The few hide scraps recovered from early-1100s contexts at Aztec pale in comparison to the intricately pieced and stitched hide artifacts recovered by Morris from later contexts at Aztec West: a child's moccasin decorated with red hematite and porcupine quillwork (fig. 8.7), a fringed piece of buckskin with porcupine quill decoration, moccasin fragments, and a painted rawhide bag. From Osborne's study, we know that the people of Mesa Verde also made extensive use of hides for moccasins, bags, shirts, pants, and ceremonial headgear and that they decorated some of these objects with red or black pigment.

People continued to wear twined and twill-plaited jog-toed sandals into the post-1150 period, but in a simpler form. Apparently, these styles of footwear became less symbolically important because the later residents of Aztec invested less time and creative energy in their production. In the case of the twined sandals, the colorful, complex designs, slit-tapestry technique, and toe loops made of hide largely disappeared, replaced by solid-colored sandals with yucca ties and coarse, raised designs on the soles. We still do not know how long twined sandals persisted at Aztec—Morris felt that they did not survive into the latest occupation of the site—but twill-plaited sandals evidently continued to be worn. At some point during this latter period, people added an even more expedient form of plaited sandal to their footwear repertoire, one with thick yucca leaves woven in diagonal 1/1 (over one, under one) interlacing or braiding. Some of the later occupants of Aztec also wore hide moccasins.

New forms of clothing and apparel that appeared during the later occupation include braided cotton sashes and painted blankets, also popular in northeastern Arizona and other areas of the northern Southwest during this time. Depictions of these garments on post-1300 kiva murals in northern Arizona and New Mexico suggest that their appearance at Aztec was tied to the introduction of new religious ceremonies. Morris's excavations at Aztec West yielded a probable cotton sash woven in 2/2 oblique interlacing (braiding) and a small,

roughly square, plain-weave cotton textile whose surface had been painted brown and red with a negatively patterned white diamond at its center. Although the Aztec example is much simpler than the intricately painted cotton blankets from the Kayenta region of northeastern Arizona, it shares the same use of negative patterning. Osborne also reported a few examples of cotton cloth painted with simple designs from Mesa Verde. Tie-dyed fabrics, known from the Kayenta region and south of the Mogollon Rim, in Arizona, were not identified at Salmon or Aztec, although one example was recently discovered in the Pueblo Bonito collections. The later occupants of Aztec colored much of their plain-weave cotton cloth red or brown, and they used twined-stitch embroidery to mend their cotton fabrics and keep them in circulation. One particularly inventive individual used this technique to create a scroll-like pattern on cotton cloth.

Hundreds of people lived and died at the Salmon and Aztec pueblos. Each morning, the residents of these communities awoke and donned particular articles of clothing, depending on the season and what activities the day held in store. Work in the village or fields, a hunting or trading expedition, a winter excursion, a meeting of political leaders, a religious ceremony, an initiation, a wedding—each would have required a different selection of clothing and ornamentation. Of the thousands of garments worn and discarded by the people of Salmon and Aztec, only a small number survive. Yet from the relatively few complete articles and more numerous fragments that have been recovered, we can begin to appreciate the complexity and beauty of this clothing and how colorful these villages would have been when home to Ancestral Pueblo people. More than seven hundred years later, our perception of their lives is immeasurably richer because of these glimpses into what they wore.

Ancestral Pueblo Pottery of the Middle San Juan Region

Lori Stephens Reed

Something about the stark beauty of winter—the angled sunlight, snow-covered landscape, and desire for warmth—pulls my thoughts and imagination into another, distant time. Bundled up in layers to keep the cold at bay, I take a walk through the massive stone labyrinth of rooms and kivas that comprise the Chacoan great house at Aztec Ruins National Monument. In the winter months, tourist visitation drops dramatically, and the resulting silence engulfs me as I slowly make my way through the rooms at the back of the pueblo, noting thousand-year-old ceilings over my head, before emerging into the open plaza. It is within this silence that I can imagine the low din of ancient voices and laughter, the crackling of flames in a fire pit, the sharp cry of an infant, or the telling of a story, all connecting me to the people who once lived within these walls. Using my imagination, unbound by time, I can feel a tangible connection to an Ancestral Pueblo past that engulfs my senses. I let it sink into my mind for a bit. As I walk slowly back to the visitor center on a lightly snow-covered path, breathing in the cold air, snowflakes fall to the ground in front of me. But my thoughts linger on the connections between the Aztec great house and other ancestral places on the landscape of human experience and accomplishment.

Moving into the warmth of the museum brings me back to the present and jolts me into remembering the long list of tasks ahead of me for the day. After a walk through the great house, however, I always feel an overwhelming sense of gratitude for the fact that I get to come to work every day in such a magnificent place. I glance at the clock, realizing I must get back to my work of photographing and analyzing pottery in the museum storage room.

The items on display in the museum at Aztec Ruins National Monument are only a fraction of the vast number of objects created and used by generations of people who lived at the great house. Each ceramic bowl, basket, or stone ax is a unique example of the ingenuity and creativity of the artisan who made it, and each piece contains its own story. Museums generally display only the most complete and well-preserved pieces, which represent a very small percentage of the artifacts recovered by archaeologists. For every whole pot on exhibit in a museum, there are tens of thousands of pieces of pottery (potsherds), chipped stone, and other objects that may not be of exhibit quality but are nevertheless full of information that the archaeologist can glean through various analytical techniques. You might ask, What sorts of information can be gathered from an examination of thousands of potsherds? Even the broken items have stories to tell.

Ancient Pueblo people had made pottery for many centuries before the great houses were built. As they began to grow beans in the 400s CE, they needed vessels in which to slowly simmer the beans. Over the centuries, potters in the Southwest both perfected their craft and developed new innovations in food storage and cooking vessels for growing populations. In addition to its everyday uses, pottery became a medium for artistic expression and for meeting social obligations through gift giving, feasting, and exchange.

As generations of Pueblo potters experimented with local resources in the Four Corners region, they developed different pottery wares to meet their needs. The term *grayware* is generally used to describe the undecorated utility pots that were made for cooking and storage.

Pottery with a white or gray surface and decorated with designs painted in black, brown, or red-brown pigments is referred to as whiteware or black-on-white ware. Both gray- and whiteware pottery types were produced by households to meet their everyday needs, but in some instances these types were also produced by specialists in larger numbers than needed by their individual household. Whereas gray- and whiteware pottery was made by most households, pottery with a red surface and black-painted designs was also made by specialists in only a few areas of the northern Southwest.

The Middle San Juan region was affiliated with the Chacoan culture and was a center of great-house construction as early as the 900s. Much of the research and literature on the region has concentrated on the great-house architecture at Salmon and Aztec Pueblos. The two enormous great houses there were unique in the Middle San Juan and were built just as Chaco itself was in the last decades of its cultural florescence. Salmon and Aztec were built in large part by craftsmen from Chaco, which explains the high-quality materials and fine workmanship of these massive great houses, as well as their endurance to the present time. Steve Lekson has proposed that Salmon and Aztec were built to accommodate the relocation of elite individuals or families and religious specialists from Chaco Canyon to a new northern capital in the early 1100s. Paul Reed and Gary Brown have elaborated on this perspective and concluded that Salmon and Aztec were two of the most important Chacoan colonies (see chapters 3 and 4).

Detailed analyses of pottery, textiles, architecture, and other items are part of the vast amount of information archaeologists use to interpret the past. As I carefully remove a pottery bowl from its secure place in the storage cabinet of the museum, my mind wanders again to the distant past. I feel the weight of the bowl in my hands and take in the beauty of the elaborately painted design on its interior. Each stroke of the brush is visible, and the exterior surface has a slightly undulating texture where impressions of the potter's fingers lingered in the wet clay, even after she had rubbed it with a polishing stone. I imagine the potter collecting the clay for this pot from a nearby outcrop, possibly along an arroyo cutbank. Her oldest daughter may have tagged along on her first excursion to collect the crumbly rocks from the river terrace near Aztec, which would be ground into coarse grains and added to the wet clay. After collecting these materials, mother and daughter would have hauled their heavy baskets of clay and broken rocks back to a shady spot by the fast-flowing Animas River to begin mixing the clay with water. Although in my imagination the potter is female, some ethnographic studies show that pottery was also made by men.

The making of a pot involves many steps, beginning with collecting the materials, mixing the raw clay with water, giving the mixture ample time to cure, and adding crushed rocks or potsherds as temper to give the clay added strength. All pottery in the New World was hand formed prior to the arrival of the Spanish, who brought the pottery wheel. Ancestral Pueblo potters used the coil-and-scrape method to make their pottery. The potter made a flat disk of clay and put it into a basket or the bottom of a broken pot for support. She made the walls of the bowl or jar by layering rolled coils or ropes of clay and pinching them into place. As she built the walls of the vessel, the potter used a tool such as a broken potsherd or a piece of gourd, wood, or stone to scrape the coil junctures and thin the vessel walls. Using the same technique, she would scrape and smooth both the interior and exterior surfaces of the vessel before applying a painted design.

Prior to roughly 900, painted designs on white- and redware pots were applied directly to the scraped and smoothed surface of the vessel. After that time, however, potters began applying a watery solution of clay, called slip, to a vessel's surface before painting it. This solution generally gave the painted surface a more consistent color, which would contrast with the black-painted designs. Potters made pigments either by cooking down various plants, such as beeweed, or by grinding certain minerals, such as hematite, and adding water to create a thick paint. The real test of the potter's training and skill came with the firing of the finished items in a kiln, which was usually a pit dug into the soil and lined with flat pieces of sandstone. All of the effort and artistry put into a finished vessel was dependent upon a potter's successful control of the immense heat and flow of oxygen within the kiln itself. Ancestral Pueblo potters were

Figure 9.1. A Mesa Verde black-on-white bowl recovered from Kiva D at Aztec West Ruin by Earl Morris. Note the dots along the rim and the lines of variable thickness encircling the interior of the bowl; these are two of the primary characteristics of Mesa Verde style. Courtesy of the Division of Anthropology, American Museum of Natural History (AMNH 29.0/6745), Lori Reed, photographer.

masters of their firing technology and were able to create consistent gray-, white-, and redware pots over many generations.

While holding the beautiful painted bowl in my hands, I think about all of the talent and skill that went into making this single piece of pottery. Looking through the microscope at the bottom surface of the bowl, I can see little fragments of the rock temper exposed through abrasion, where the bowl was repeatedly placed on and moved over a hard surface during its use. These exposed rock grains have a specific texture, and I recognize the combination of quartz and dark minerals, which indicates a local origin for this bowl. The rocks that were crushed and added to the clay were probably collected from nearby river terraces or mesas. The deep black geometric design on the interior of the bowl was carefully painted using a brush of yucca fiber, and the paint was most likely made from the beeweed plant collected during the month of August, when it blooms.

As I examine the bowl more closely, I begin to see all of the characteristic attributes that I associate with a pot made in the Middle San Juan, perhaps by a potter from the monumental three-story great house we call Aztec West, or one of the small community pueblos nearby. In addition to the rock fragments visible on the worn surface of the bowl base, I also see that the slip covering the bowl is off-white and has a chalky appearance, the pigment used to paint the design is organic (derived from beeweed), and the painted design includes little dots or ticks on the rim and parallel lines of multiple thicknesses encircling the interior of the bowl just below the rim (fig. 9.1). Collectively, these clues indicate that the bowl fits into the Mesa Verde style, dating between 1175 and 1290.

Designs on pottery, in rock art, and in other media make cultural changes visible in the archaeological record, and each whole pot or potsherd provides an abundance of information concerning when and where the pot was made and how it was used. Archaeologists use this information to study chronological changes at a pueblo and to understand the activities that occurred there. After the decline of Chaco in the mid-1100s, painted pottery styles went through a major shift in the configuration and orientation of their designs, and Mesa Verde–style pottery became the hallmark whiteware in the Four Corners region. These changes in pottery designs represent in a visible way the social, political, and religious reorganization that took place from the Chacoan to post-Chacoan eras.

In the Middle San Juan region, pottery is one of several windows into the past through which the influence of Chacoan culture is visible. At the earliest great houses in the Middle San Juan, such as Point Site and Aztec North, a significant amount of the pottery was brought in from the Chaco Canyon area and also from the Chuska Valley, directly west of Chaco. In fact, people in the Chuska Valley were intricately connected to Chaco, and at some great houses in Chaco Canyon more than half of the cooking pots were brought in from the Chuska Valley. Chuska Valley potters added a crushed igneous rock temper to their clays, known as trachyte basalt, which often created a distinctive shiny green color on the surface of cooking pots and can also be seen in the clay body of broken potsherds examined with a microscope. Although not as abundant at Middle San Juan great houses, amounts of pottery from the Chuska Valley definitely increased as connections to Chaco Canyon developed and local great houses were built.

Prior to 900, pottery from the Chaco Canyon and Chuska Valley regions was relatively scarce in the Middle San Juan, and most of the imported pottery was from the Mesa Verde region to the northwest. Although they felt the influence of the Mesa Verde region between about 600 and 900, potters in the Middle San Juan marched to their own beat and created unique pottery wares. It was during the late 900s, however, that the influence of Chaco Canyon was first felt in the Middle San Juan. Point Site, located on the south side of the San Juan River near Farmington, was probably one of the earliest great houses built by local people. Based on its architecture, archaeologists believe Point Site may have been built as a local copy of the multistoried great houses in Chaco Canyon. Within just a few generations, great houses dotted the landscape along the La Plata, Animas, and San Juan Rivers, serving both as the centers of local communities and as ties to the cultural developments in

Chaco Canyon. Recent field-school excavations by San Juan College at the Point great house on B-Square Ranch have revealed pottery dating to the late 900s, much of which appears to have been imported from the Chaco and Chuska regions.

Pots from the Mogollon region south and west of the modern pueblo of Zuni were part of the exotic suite of items linked to Chaco Canyon. In contrast to the gray- and whiteware pottery produced in the Middle San Juan and other regions of the Four Corners, Mogollon pottery had a distinctive brown color and often a very shiny polish on the interiors of bowls. Mogollon potters used a firing technology significantly different from that of potters in the Four Corners region, and Mogollon pots are easily recognized.

White Mountain Red Ware pottery, made just north of the Mogollon region, became common in great-house communities during the late 1000s. People traded this pottery throughout the Chacoan network and brought many vessels into Middle San Juan great houses. This redware connection began during the Chacoan period and continued even after the decline of Chaco Canyon's influence, during the rise of Aztec as a center of social and ritual power. At Aztec in the 1100s–1200s, White Mountain Red Ware was the most common redware pottery, particularly a form known as St. Johns Polychrome: large bowls with designs painted in black on the interior surfaces and white on the exterior surfaces. Residents of Salmon Pueblo traded for many of these vessels.

After placing the bowl I have been examining back onto the museum storage shelf, I glance across to the other shelves in the storage cabinet, noticing the variety of pottery forms represented. Some of the items are classic shapes associated with the Chacoan period, including "sharp-shouldered" pitchers, cylinder jars, small shallow bowls, and human-shaped figures, or effigies (fig. 9.2). Recent research and analysis conducted on these special pottery items, especially the cylinder jars, have revealed some surprising results.

Cylinder jars, including a large cache found in a single room at Pueblo Bonito in Chaco Canyon, were of special significance for the Chacoan people (fig. 9.3). Archaeologist Patricia Crown has recently discovered that cylinder jars from Pueblo Bonito were used to hold

Lori Stephens Reed

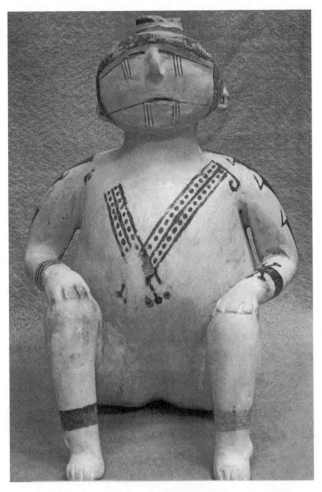

Figure 9.2. Human-effigy vessels such as this one from Aztec Ruins are rare and were made primarily during the Chaco era. Although reconstructed using plaster fill to create the full shape of the effigy, the original painted pieces of the effigy show elaborate designs painted on the body, arms, and face of the figure. Courtesy of the Division of Anthropology, American Museum of Natural History (AMNH 29.1/3209), Lori Reed, photographer.

Figure 9.3. A Chaco black-on-white cylinder jar from Room 28 at Pueblo Bonito. Research has shown that these jars were used in the preparation and serving of a cacao drink consumed primarily at great houses in Chaco Canyon, but also at other great houses. Fragments of two cylinder jars have been identified in the Aztec Ruins collections. Courtesy of the Division of Anthropology, American Museum of Natural History (catalog no. H/3229) and Dorothy Washburn, James Garber, photographer.

cacao (raw chocolate) imported from Mesoamerica, more than a thousand miles to the south. The linkage between cacao and cylinder jars at Pueblo Bonito is significant because it suggests that these special containers were used for a ritual similar to ones practiced among ancient Mesoamerican cultures. Cylinder jars are relatively scarce outside of Chaco Canyon but have been identified in several outlying great houses. Archaeologists have identified two fragments in the Aztec collection, and one of these was submitted to Crown for residue analysis, though it did not show evidence of cacao. The presence of two cylinder jars at the Aztec West great

house suggests, however, that the ritual associated with this special jar form was brought to Aztec from Chaco. Cacao residue has also been found in three mugs from Aztec West. This finding is significant because it demonstrates that Chacoan rituals surrounding cacao persisted beyond Chaco Canyon great houses.

The painted designs on cylinder jars, pitchers, and other vessel forms also indicate connections to Chaco Canyon. One of the most common design motifs painted on pottery during the Chacoan period consisted of a ribbon filled with straight or obliquely oriented hatching. Although hatching was a common theme, researcher

Figure 9.4. A small shallow Chaco black-on-white bowl from Salmon Ruin that has the distinctive hatched Chaco Design Symmetry painted on the interior. Courtesy of the Salmon Ruins Museum (FS 32828), Lori Reed, photographer.

Dorothy Washburn has identified a specific symmetry to some of the hatched designs that were most common in Chaco Canyon, in Pueblo Bonito, and on many of the cylinder jars, which she calls Chaco Design Symmetry. This symmetry was quite complex, involved the execution of the overall motif with a single continuous line, and was not easily copied. During a collaborative analysis, Washburn and I were able to identify locally made pots from both the Salmon and Aztec great houses that exhibited Chaco Design Symmetry. On some of the vessels the symmetry was perfect, suggesting that these items were made by a potter from Chaco Canyon who had relocated to Salmon or Aztec (fig. 9.4). In contrast, some vessels had flawed symmetry, suggesting that the potter was attempting to copy Chaco-style designs or was not experienced with the more complex symmetry pattern. One cylinder-jar fragment from Aztec has a hatched design painted on the exterior surface that fits the criteria for Chaco Design Symmetry. This cylinder jar was also made locally in the Middle San Juan, likely at Aztec, and may have been made by a Chacoan migrant or her descendant with the intent of continuing the traditions of the past.

One additional attribute of Chacoan pottery was copied or emulated by local potters in the Middle San Juan. As I have mentioned, potters would often add a layer of slip to the surface of a pot before applying the painted design. Potters of different traditions had specific sources for slip clays and unique ways of mixing and applying the slip. One of the calling cards of Chaco black-on-white pottery is the distinctive application style of a white slip. Chacoan potters applied the slip so thinly that the original gray surface of the vessel was partially visible beneath the "washy" slip. As I examine pottery in the Aztec collections, I look specifically for this white washy slip as a prime characteristic of Chacoan pottery or influence.

Local Middle San Juan potters, in contrast, generally applied a white slip more thickly so that the pottery surface underneath was not visible. This difference in slip application is easily seen on a whole pot or even on a small potsherd. At the Salmon and Aztec great houses, potters used local clays and applied slips in the washy Chacoan style for a short time during the early 1100s. Some of their vessels also have the complex Chaco Design Symmetry. The distinctive Chacoan architectural characteristics of Salmon and Aztec, along with the quantity of exotic trade items and the ceramics I have discussed, indicate that these great houses were built by Chacoan migrants. Local folks helped build Chacoan-style great houses and copied Chacoan-style designs and techniques in their pottery to link themselves to the powerful cultural and ritual system centered in Chaco Canyon.

By the time that Aztec was flourishing in the 1130s, the influence of Chaco Canyon was declining due to social, religious, and climatic changes, and people in the Middle San Juan shifted their attention to local concerns. Pottery at Salmon and Aztec and at other great-house communities in the Middle San Juan began to lose much of its Chacoan character as the people reorganized themselves and implemented new ideas—new ceremonies, social networks, and leadership. By the mid-1100s, nearly all the Chacoan pottery styles were gone. With the exception of the occasional bowl with washy slip or a sharp-shouldered pitcher, pottery forms and designs went through a series of rapid changes toward the Mesa

Lori Stephens Reed

Figure 9.5. A Mesa Verde black-on-white mug recovered from Kiva D at Aztec West Ruin by Earl Morris. Along with cylinder jars from the Chaco era, mugs similar to this one from Aztec Ruins and other great houses were used to drink caffeinated beverages such as the one made from cacao and holly. Courtesy of the Division of Anthropology, American Museum of Natural History (AMNH 29.0/6755), Lori Reed, photographer.

Verde–style bowls and mugs that would define the 1200s (fig. 9.5). Since the time that Earl Morris excavated Aztec West in the early twentieth century, archaeologists have speculated on this change from Chaco-style to Mesa Verde–style pottery and culture. The changes that occurred within the pottery and architectural styles were dramatic enough to have prompted Morris and others to interpret them as representing the replacement of Chacoan people by people from Mesa Verde. Research over the last decade at numerous sites in the Middle San Juan, however, indicates that Chacoan people were not replaced by people from Mesa Verde, but rather that local Middle San Juan culture was transformed as the result of Chaco's decline and Aztec's rise to regional power.

As I scatter a bag of potsherds over my work table and begin to sort through them, my mind is filled with thoughts of cacao, cylinder jars, mugs, hatched designs with intricate symmetry, and exotic redware bowls. Picking up the broken fragment of a St. Johns Polychrome bowl with a bright red-slipped surface, a complex design of solid lines and hatched ribbons on the interior, and big bold circles painted in white on the exterior, I move toward the microscope and say out loud, "Tell me your story."

The Intertwined Histories of the Chaco, Middle San Juan, and Mesa Verde Regions

Mark D. Varien

The construction of new pueblos at Salmon and Aztec, followed shortly thereafter by the demise of Chaco Canyon, was an event of unprecedented importance in the history of Pueblo people. By the late 1000s CE, after centuries of development, the great houses built along a twelve-mile stretch of Chaco Canyon coalesced into the political and ceremonial center of the Ancestral Pueblo world. Just a few decades later, by about 1140, great-house construction at Chaco ceased. During this same interval, people from Chaco directed the construction of new great houses at Salmon and Aztec: the largest great houses by far built outside of Chaco Canyon. Clearly, the late eleventh and early twelfth centuries were times of momentous change, and the repercussions that accompanied the demise of Chaco and rise of Salmon and Aztec must have reverberated throughout the Puebloan world and beyond—especially so in the central Mesa Verde region to the north.

Archaeologists have speculated on the relationship between the Chaco, Middle San Juan, and Mesa Verde regions since great houses and cliff dwellings were first discovered more than a century ago (fig. 10.1). How did these areas interact, and how did they become major centers of the Puebloan world? Did the demise of Chaco and the relatively sudden appearance of Salmon and Aztec affect the inhabitants of the Mesa Verde region? Conversely, did Mesa Verde people contribute to the dramatic events that unfolded in the Chaco Canyon and Middle San Juan regions? Were the inhabitants of these three areas the same people, or were they from different cultural groups?

Answering these questions is no easy task and requires unraveling the long-standing ties between the three regions. But archaeologists are, if nothing else, a tenacious lot, and they've uncovered a great deal of evidence to show how settlements in the three regions were intertwined. This cumulative evidence can be woven into a fascinating story, which, like all archaeological tales, raises as many questions as it answers.

I trace the connection between Chaco Canyon and Mesa Verde to a period much earlier than most of my colleagues. I believe this relationship dates back to at least the early seventh century, a period that archaeologists call Basketmaker III. Both regions were curiously underpopulated in the preceding period, the Basketmaker II era, when an agricultural lifeway was first established in the Puebloan area. Then, relatively suddenly, Basketmaker III people settled both the Chaco Canyon and central Mesa Verde areas in larger numbers for the first time. When they did so they also created new institutions that integrated what had previously been disparate groups who likely spoke different languages and who had distinct histories. Their innovations included the formation of larger and more permanent settlements, which I call villages, and the construction of the first buildings for group ceremony: great kivas. Basketmaker III villages with great kivas are rare in the Puebloan world, but archaeologists have found them in both the Chaco Canyon and Mesa Verde areas. We currently understand almost nothing about the connection between the two areas during this pivotal period, but we do know that these cultural institutions—villages and great kivas—persisted in both areas, if sporadically, for the next seven centuries.

An important connection between the Mesa Verde and Chaco Canyon areas emerged again in the mid- to

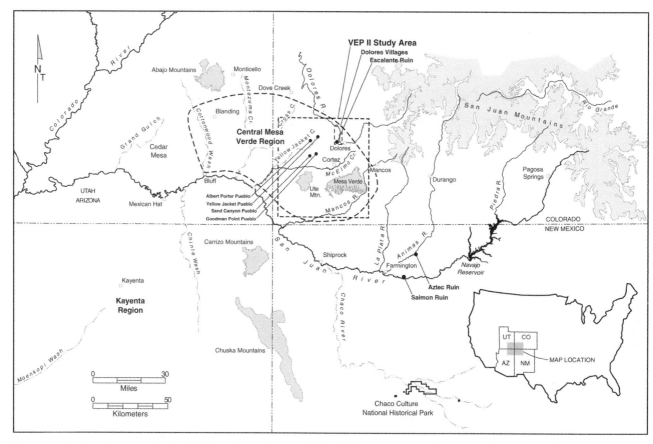

Figure 10.1. A regional map showing the VEP II study area, the central Mesa Verde region, Aztec, Salmon, and Chaco Culture National Historical Park. Courtesy of the Crow Canyon Archaeological Center.

late ninth century, the time when great-house construction at Chaco Canyon began with three crescent-shaped buildings: Una Vida on the east end of the canyon, Peñasco Blanco on the west, and Pueblo Bonito in the center. At the same time, similar buildings were being constructed in the central Mesa Verde region, with the largest and most important being McPhee Village in the Dolores River Valley (fig. 10.2). In fact, the Dolores Valley contained the densest concentration of the largest sites anywhere in the Ancestral Pueblo world at this time (fig. 10.3). What happened next in the two regions was completely different: the Dolores Valley was largely depopulated by 900, while great houses in Chaco Canyon grew in size and number throughout the tenth century.

Most archaeologists focus on the depopulation of the central Mesa Verde area as the factor most important for understanding the development of Chaco, arguing

that people moved from Mesa Verde to the San Juan Basin and provided the demographic foundation that supported the rise of the Chacoan polity. Just as important, I believe, was the interaction between the Chaco and Mesa Verde areas in the ninth century, when great houses first appeared. Elsewhere in the world, competition between centers such as these stimulated the development of greater social and political complexity, and I wonder if this dynamic jump-started Chaco's early development as well.

Events in the Chaco and Mesa Verde areas diverged for the entire tenth century and for most of the eleventh; Chaco grew and its influence spread, while population levels in the central Mesa Verde region dropped and remained relatively low. Then population levels in the central Mesa Verde region grew dramatically during the period when we see the first Chaco-like great houses constructed in the area.

Mark D. Varien

Figure 10.2. A U-shaped roomblock at McPhee Village, Dolores River Valley, southwestern Colorado. Courtesy of the Crow Canyon Archaeological Center.

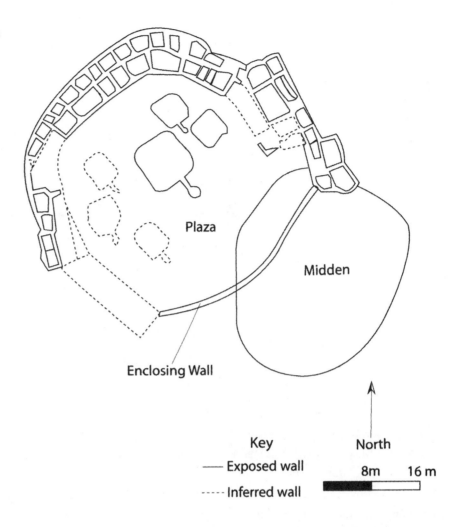

Plaza

Midden

Enclosing Wall

Key
—— Exposed wall
---- Inferred wall

North

8m   16 m

Figure 10.3. A photograph of site 5MT5107 illustrating an example of a U-shaped roomblock with associated pit structures, which was excavated during the Dolores Archaeology Program. Site 5107 is one of the sites that form the McPhee Village community cluster in the Dolores River Valley. Courtesy of the Crow Canyon Archaeological Center, Richard Wilshusen, photographer.

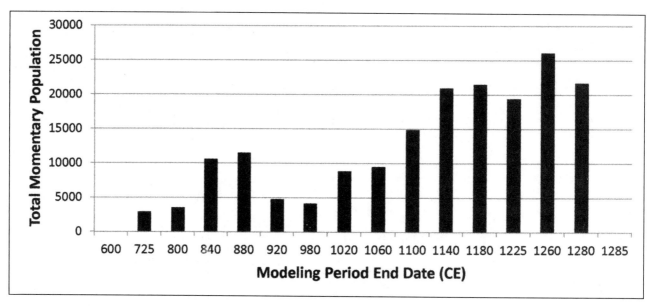

Figure 10.4. A graph showing the population history of the VEP study area in the central Mesa Verde region. Courtesy of the Crow Canyon Archaeological Center.

We know this thanks to a recent research initiative I am a part of: the Village Ecodynamics Project, or VEP. A team of VEP archaeologists has recently reconstructed population levels for our study area in the Mesa Verde region of southwestern Colorado (fig. 10.4). We have compiled the information for all recorded sites, which number more than eighteen thousand. Our analysis has focused on residential sites with houses, and we analyzed these to determine when they were occupied and how many people lived in them.

VEP archaeologists have also tracked the first appearance of Chacoan-style great houses in the Mesa Verde region. Some sites with great houses show traces of earlier occupation, but I believe construction of the actual great houses did not begin until around 1080, about the same time Chacoans built Salmon in the Middle San Juan (see chapter 3). Many Mesa Verde great houses were remodeled in the early 1100s—the same time that Aztec West was constructed (see chapter 4)— and many new great houses, like Escalante Ruin, were built in the Mesa Verde region at this time. Like Salmon and Aztec—and contrary to events at Chaco—some Mesa Verde great houses had new construction and remained occupied after 1140 and well into the 1200s.

Given the long-standing ties between the regions, I find it curious that Chacoan influence took so long to expand into the Mesa Verde region. Further, the fact that this influence spread at the same time that Salmon was built and Aztec emerged as a major center makes me wonder whether this expansion into the Mesa Verde country is tied to Chaco itself or, instead, to the development of these new and important centers on the Middle San Juan.

Many archaeologists, especially the editors of this volume, have contributed to our understanding of the Middle San Juan settlement system and the emergence of Aztec as a major center, but Steve Lekson's book *The Chaco Meridian* makes this argument with the greatest flourish. Archaeologists debate the details of Lekson's arguments, but I think there is near consensus on the two most salient points: elites from Chaco Canyon directed the construction of Aztec West, and after Chaco's demise the larger Aztec complex filled the void as the largest multisite center in the Puebloan world.

Lekson argues that an elite class of leaders lived at Aztec and ruled over a domain that was smaller than the one controlled by Chaco but a sizable area nonetheless. He suggests it encompassed the entire northern San Juan

Mark D. Varien

region. On this point few agree, and some archaeologists have mounted evidence to argue that Aztec's influence was limited to a smaller area focused on the Middle San Juan. Archaeologists disagree largely because using archaeological data to measure political control is inherently difficult. We need more studies focused on this problem; for now, we can only assess the extent of Aztec's influence with the bits and pieces of evidence available.

Once again, population reconstructions are a useful place to start. Researchers at Archaeology Southwest have recently compiled population estimates for the entire Southwest. Their study begins at 1200, and it shows that two population centers had developed in the northern Southwest by this time, one centered on Aztec in the Middle San Juan and the other on the central Mesa Verde region in southwestern Colorado. Donna Glowacki's research refines this study and shows that population had concentrated in the two areas by the middle 1100s. The VEP population estimates for southwestern Colorado show that this area grew dramatically after 1150 and peaked at more than twenty-six thousand people in the middle 1200s. Reed and Brown document similar trends for the Middle San Juan: population there also grew after 1150 and similarly peaked in the middle 1200s. But the Middle San Juan population peaked at about six thousand people, so population size in this area was much smaller than in the neighboring central Mesa Verde region. Glowacki's work also shows a less densely populated zone between the Middle San Juan and central Mesa Verde regions, as if there were a buffer zone between the two areas, however this needs to be verified by additional survey.

Glowacki's study also documents the exchange of pottery vessels between the two regions, so we know that the people living in both areas interacted. This interaction resulted in the two areas developing a shared tradition, as reflected in similarities in architecture, pottery, and other artifacts. This shared tradition makes the northern San Juan region as a whole increasingly distinctive when compared to the rest of the Puebloan world after 1150. One element of this new tradition was a new form of public architecture—multiple-walled structures. These are buildings with concentric walls, in which the spaces between the walls are divided by cross walls, creating many smaller rooms, and which usually, but not always, contain a kiva or kivas in the center.

Pueblo people may have used these buildings in different ways; however, excavation in a few of them shows evidence for both domestic and ritual activities. This evidence has led Scott Ortman to suggest that they were special houses used by leaders living in the villages where they were located and that on occasion these leaders sponsored ceremonies in them. Access to the kivas in these buildings was more restricted, and their size would have limited the number of people who attended rituals held in those chambers, which means the rituals were more exclusive when compared to the inclusive, communal rituals that occurred in great kivas. I believe the appearance of multiple-walled structures signals an important change in leadership and ritual practices in the post-Chacoan world.

Almost all multiple-walled structures are found in either the Middle San Juan or the central Mesa Verde region of southwestern Colorado. Lekson suggests that the area where these structures are found provides a measure of the extent of Aztec influence. Glowacki's research illustrates the regional distribution of these structures and reveals several interesting patterns: many more of these buildings were built in the central Mesa Verde region, circular tri-wall structures are almost exclusively at Aztec in the Middle San Juan (there is only one in southwestern Colorado), and D-shaped bi-wall structures are only found in southwestern Colorado (fig. 10.5). These differences may seem insignificant— bi-walls versus tri-walls and D shapes versus circular buildings—but buildings were important symbols, both in terms of their permanence and their ability to communicate meaning in relatively unambiguous ways. These differences suggest to me that the Middle San Juan and central Mesa Verde regions were not integrated into a single polity, a point that is, for me, reinforced by the fact that the D-shaped structures became more numerous in the middle and late 1200s when the central Mesa Verde region reached its population peak.

How did these differences between the two regions, which I believe intensified through time after 1140, play

3D Reconstruction

Figure 10.5. A three-dimensional reconstruction and map of the D-shaped building at Sand Canyon Pueblo. Courtesy of the Crow Canyon Archaeological Center.

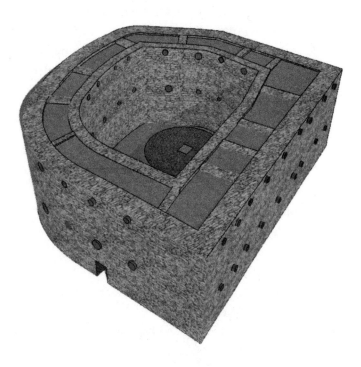

Site 5MT765, Excavated Portion of Architectural Block 1500

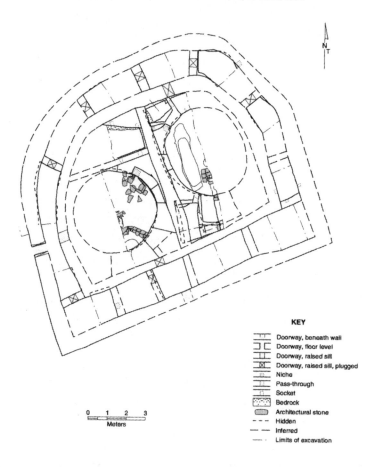

N

KEY

	Doorway, beneath wall
	Doorway, floor level
	Doorway, raised sill
	Doorway, raised sill, plugged
	Niche
	Pass-through
	Socket
	Bedrock
	Architectural stone
- - -	Hidden
— —	Inferred
—·—	Limits of excavation

0 1 2 3
Meters

out in the lives of the Pueblo people who lived there? Examination of the evidence for the extent of conflict and violence provides a partial answer to this question. In one study, Tim Kohler and Kathryn Turner examined the ratio of males to females in burial populations in the Chaco, Middle San Juan, and central Mesa Verde regions. Their analysis reveals times when this ratio was significantly out of balance. They found an unusually high proportion of females in both the Chaco population during the eleventh century and the Middle San Juan population in the thirteenth century. One explanation is that conflict initiated from the Chaco and Aztec areas included the capture of women. This interpretation is supported by evidence from the central Mesa Verde region during the thirteenth century: significantly fewer females than would be expected characterized the burial populations in this area at this time. It appears that women from the central Mesa Verde region were being taken to the Middle San Juan as captives.

Supporting this interpretation is a study of burials from sites in the lower La Plata River Valley, just above its confluence with the San Juan. These burials were removed and analyzed in consultation with American Indian tribes because the sites were being destroyed by an expansion of a highway right-of-way. Debra Martin and her colleagues showed that females at these sites were buried in two contrasting ways: the careful interment of women who often had accompanying grave offerings, versus the casual disposal of females whose interments lacked grave goods. The females buried casually showed multiple signs of skeletal trauma, likely from having been abused throughout their lives. Martin believes these women suffered because they were captives.

In another important study, Kohler and his colleagues synthesized all evidence for skeletal trauma due to conflict from the VEP study area in southwestern Colorado and created an index to track how the level of conflict changed through time. A powerful analytical tool, the index can be used to see if the changing levels of conflict correspond to changes in population size, changes in agricultural yields, or other factors.

Kohler and colleagues found that between 600 and 1280, high levels of conflict were relatively rare, typically sporadic and short-lived, with one important exception: consistently high levels of conflict occurred during a sustained interval between 1060 and 1180. The highest level of conflict occurred from 1140 to 1180, when 89 percent of individuals show skeletal trauma from conflict. The next highest level occurred from 1060 to 1100 (54 percent), and the period between 1100 and 1140 was also high (41 percent). The final period, 1260 to 1280, when people were migrating from the region, had a similarly high level, 42 percent.

This study also tallies the kind of trauma to human bone that archaeologists call "extreme processing," which refers to skeletons that were taken apart and broken into tiny pieces. This behavior goes beyond killing people and processing their remains for a utilitarian purpose—that is, for food. Instead, I believe the extreme processing was intended to send a message, and while I can't decode the specifics, it seems likely it served as a means of intimidation. Almost all cases of extreme processing date between 1020 and 1180, with the vast majority occurring in an even shorter interval: 1130 to 1160.

Archaeologists commonly explain conflict in ancient societies as the result of competition for resources, which could be intensified by increasing population, decreasing agricultural yields due to deteriorating climate, or a combination of the two. An example would be the drier-than-normal conditions during much of the period from 1140 to 1180. Surprisingly, Kohler and his colleagues have shown only a weak relationship between these factors and increased conflict in the Mesa Verde region during the entire Puebloan sequence. Instead, their study suggests that cultural factors played an important role.

The sustained period of higher violence between 1060 and 1180 corresponds to the intrusion of Chaco/Aztec influence in the region, the demise of Chaco, and establishment of Aztec as Chaco's heir. I believe these events played an important role in producing this sustained period of high conflict. This period included the time during which residents of the central Mesa Verde region resisted the initial efforts by the people of Chaco or Aztec to exert their influence in the region, as well as a particularly contentious and violent episode that accompanied Chaco's demise and Aztec's rise to prominence. Kohler's index shows a decline in conflict between 1180 and 1260, but the research on sex ratios suggests that women were still being taken as captives during this period. We are left to wonder how this sustained conflict tore at the fabric of Puebloan society. Surely it was a factor that shaped the dramatic changes in settlement patterns during the 1200s and contributed to the region's depopulation by 1280.

The long-standing and intertwined histories of the people living in the Chaco Canyon, Middle San Juan, and Mesa Verde regions, along with this evidence for conflict, raise the question of whether the individuals living in these three areas were the same people or of different groups. In trying to answer this question, archaeologists have long equated artifacts with people. For example, many scholars have proposed that different cultural groups lived in Chaco Canyon and Mesa Verde based on the fact that the two areas were characterized by distinct types of buildings and, to a degree, different styles of pottery. Several implicit assumptions underlie this perspective: the notion that Ancestral Pueblo people lived their lives in relatively small and bounded areas, that they learned how to construct buildings and manufacture pottery in the areas where they lived, and that these traditions only changed when groups moved from one area to another. It was this basic line of thinking that led Earl Morris to conclude that people from Chaco initiated construction at Aztec, but that emigrants from the Mesa Verde region eventually replaced the Chacoans.

However, archaeologists have come to view the equation that links artifacts and people as too simplistic. Over time we've learned that people, artifacts, and ideas were constantly moving throughout the Ancestral Pueblo world. Rather than marking group identity in a straightforward manner, building styles and pottery decoration conveyed meanings, and people manipulated these meanings as they pursued their social and political goals. For example, the first Chacoan-style buildings in the Mesa Verde area may have been built, not by people who moved there from Chaco Canyon, but instead by local leaders who copied Chacoan-style architecture to draw on this potent symbolism and legitimize their claims to leadership (figs. 10.6a and 10.6b). The picture for archaeologists has gotten much more complex but also much more interesting.

Today, most archaeologists have a different interpretation of the changes in architecture and pottery style that were once used to recognize separate Chacoan and Mesa Verde groups. They argue instead that a single group with a widespread culture originally occupied the Chaco Canyon, Middle San Juan, and Mesa Verde regions, and that evolving styles of building and pottery design were simply changes that occurred over time in all three areas.

I wonder if there is an element of truth to both perspectives. Today, twenty-two different Pueblo groups live in New Mexico, Arizona, and Texas. These people share a generally similar culture but also comprise groups who have different histories and who speak six different languages: Hopi, Zuni, Keres, Towa, Tewa, and Tiwa. People from these different groups interacted with each other for more than two thousand years, producing a generally similar Puebloan culture that they share; however, during this same interval, they also preserved their historic and linguistic diversity. A culture shared by people who belong to diverse groups is an integral part of the Pueblo world today and almost certainly was in the past as well.

In a pioneering study, Ortman has used the methods of physical anthropology to better understand the genetic history of Ancestral Pueblo people, rather than relying on artifacts alone. His work is based on research that shows how the shapes of human faces can serve as measures of genetic proximity: people with similarly shaped faces share a genetic history. Ortman analyzed the facial measurements of individuals from a large portion of the Ancestral Pueblo world and found that people living in the Mesa Verde region between 1000 and 1300 formed a group with people living after 1300 in the portion of the Rio Grande drainage, where the Tewa language is spoken today. Interestingly, individuals from the Chaco and Middle San Juan areas were not included in this group; instead, they formed groups with other Ancestral Pueblo peoples.

The individuals who lived in the Chaco, Middle San Juan, and Mesa Verde areas were all Pueblo people. But Ortman's study suggests that they also made up diverse groups who likely had shared but distinct histories and who probably spoke different languages. And it's unlikely

Mark D. Varien

(a)

(b)

Figures 10.6a and 10.6b. The Cutthroat Castle (a) and Holly group (b) at Hovenweep National Monument. Located in the central Mesa Verde region near the Colorado-Utah border, these ancestral Pueblo sites were occupied during the thirteenth century immediately prior to the depopulation of the region. Courtesy of the Crow Canyon Archaeological Center, Mark Montgomery, photographer.

that each area was entirely homogenous; instead, some individuals from most Puebloan linguistic groups were probably mixed into the populations of each region. This complex social and historical tapestry helps us appreciate why a study of the Puebloan archaeological record is both challenging and rewarding.

I think the Salmon, Aztec, and the Middle San Juan region was a big deal, and it's time to recognize this area as an important center in and of itself and not as a stepchild to Chaco and Mesa Verde. It also seems clear to me that Chaco was an expansionist polity that sought to extend its influence to the highest degree possible, and Aztec, as its heir, likely pursued similar goals. The available evidence suggests to me that some people in the central Mesa Verde region embraced a relationship with these two sequential powers but that others resisted.

Our population estimates for the VEP study area decline slightly between 1180 and 1225. Were people leaving the Mesa Verde region and settling in the Middle San Juan and at Aztec, as Earl Morris believed? This scenario seems unlikely to me, given the history of conflict between the two areas, and the drop in population is so low—about eighteen hundred people—that I think decreasing fertility or increasing mortality are probably better explanations. But the idea cannot be entirely dismissed. Perhaps this decline included a few people from the Mesa Verde area who had allied themselves with Aztec and who fled the Mesa Verde region at this time.

In contrast, central Mesa Verde's population grew so rapidly between 1225 and 1260 that no large-scale movement from the Mesa Verde area to the Middle San Juan was likely to have occurred at this time. By the mid-1200s, population peaked at more than twenty-six thousand people in the VEP study area, many times the size of the population estimates for the Middle San Juan, which must have made it even harder for Aztec to pursue any expansionist ambitions to the north. The "turbulent 1200s"—to borrow a phrase from my colleague Bill Lipe—were a time of dramatic changes in the central Mesa Verde region. Those living in the area increasingly moved out of their small family farmsteads and into larger villages, and these villages took on a form distinct to this region, another sign that the central Mesa Verde region was resisting rather than conforming to ideas that emanated from Aztec.

Almost certainly, historical links to Chaco Canyon and the contested relationship with Aztec were among the factors that shaped the way Mesa Verde society changed in the 1200s and contributed to the depopulation of the region by the end of the century.

An Acoma Perspective on the Middle San Juan Region

Theresa Pasqual

It is good to start at the beginning; it is how we do things. A long time ago, two sisters were created and lived in a place below we call Ship'apu. It was at Ship'apu that T'sitchtinaku gave language and understanding to the sisters. After being created, and after coming into knowledge, they emerged into this world. The earth was not how we know it, it was new and untouched, spongy and damp like fresh clay. Upon emergence, the sisters received everything they would need to live from their father, Uutsichti, including many different animals and plants. After the sisters parted ways, with Nautsiti going east and Iiyatik'u remaining, everything was created, our clans were created, and the weather along with their spirits were formed. This was the beginning of our people, this was your beginning.

My first encounter with this place to the north was during my grade-school years at Acoma Pueblo in west-central New Mexico. My family has lived at Acoma for generations. My father, Dziyunai, had decided that the family would take a trip north to visit Kashikatrəti, otherwise known as Mesa Verde. It would be the first time that I would set foot in the places that I heard of in the prayers and songs of my people, and it would be the first time that in our journey northward—passing through places with now familiar names like San Mateo, El Rito, Kin Nizhoni, Chaco Canyon, Salmon, and Aztec—my father would begin to tell me how these places came into being and their role in our world. We passed miles and miles of backcountry dirt roads with my father's stories and songs, songs that were sung at the pueblo during ceremony and festival, recalling places

of importance to Acoma. They told of the rain spirits that came from the north, bringing with them blessings for our people. They told of beings that lived in former worlds, their adventures and misfortunes all shaping who we would become as Acoma people. Lessons of survival, stewardship, respect, honor, and interconnectedness were woven into the details of every story and brought to life what I'm sure looked to most people like mounds of rubble, rock, and sand. With my father's stories and songs, everything came to life and was renewed (fig. 11.1).

Mid-trip, my father announced that we would take a lunch break not far from Aztec Ruins, but only after a side trip to the river. Both my parents wanted to see the great San Juan River. Water in all forms is important to all Pueblo people; my father knew this intimately as a farmer and sheepherder. He prayed daily for moisture, and he knew where to find it in the canyons where he grazed our sheep. In order to survive, out of respect to the spirits that provide this blessing, one must always offer prayers to the water to ensure its continuation, and so my father made his way to the banks of the San Juan to give thanks. I got to touch the river that day. I remember its coolness, color, and taste, and I wished we could stay longer. On the drive to Aztec my father talked about how ideal the Middle San Juan region was for the ancestors to settle, near the place of the three rivers (San Juan, Animas, and La Plata)—how rich in blessings they must have been!

After lunch, my father took us to the national monument to see the old village. It was as if we were home. The first thing that caught my eye was how large the village was and how similar in height it was to my own pueblo: three stories. The village had finished rooms, just like

Figure 11.1. Haak'u (Acoma name for their pueblo) under summer rain clouds, Acoma Pueblo, New Mexico. Courtesy of Theresa Pasqual, photographer.

our own at the pueblo, places for grinding meal, cooking, storing food, and gathering people together. It had dwelling spaces and large places of ceremony—the kivas. The walls were constructed with stone and finished on the interior the way my father had built my own mother's house. The sweetness of damp clay must have permeated the air as the walls were being plastered and the roofs constructed. In my young mind, all I could think of was "What a great place to live and play as a child!"

Next, my father took us to see the large kiva. He said that it was not always this way; that it had been reconstructed so people could imagine what it must have looked like. I sat in its coolness looking up at the roof, imagining my father's songs echoing inside, wondering what it must have been like. As a child, that's all that I would allow my mind to think of in a place such as this, afraid to be disrespectful of the spirits that occupied it. Sitting beside me, my father reminded me that these people were our people, too, that we all came from the same place, and that one

day I would understand. Little did I know it would take twenty-five years before I would understand.

Time and circumstance took me far beyond the mesas and mountains of my childhood. Like Nautsiti, I headed east in search of new worlds and experiences, far beyond the reach of my father's songs and stories. I built my life and family in a world that was far different than what I was born into. The traditional cycles of seasons and ceremonies were replaced with American icons of Santa Claus, the Easter Bunny, and pumpkins and perfectly roasted turkeys. So it went year after year, until one autumn in the early morning darkness when I received a phone call; heard my name, Shiyaichiti; and was told of my mother's passing and asked to return home. The night I returned to my mother's home, the first snow was beginning to fall, a blessing always, but almost as certain a sign (fig. 11.2).

I returned to life at the pueblo, leaving behind my fast-paced and modern world. A part of our emergence story tells of Nautsiti saying to her sister, Iiyatik'u, that she would return one day but that Iiyatik'u would not recognize her. I felt that same disconnect after many years away from home. My father, easing the loss of my mother in his own way, healing simply, wanted to reconnect to the places of his past, to the mountains and mesas of his younger days. I drove my elderly father to the places where stories became the real, tangible places of our history. Daily he would recite the names of landmarks, interpreting their meanings and purposes. Our daily journeys took us in all directions: north, west, south, and east. At the ruins of old villages he would point out the similarities of building forms to each other and to our own, and we'd look at sherds of pottery, reminiscing about my mother's own skills, remembering special places for pigment and clay. My own love for

stone came from my father: he was attracted to broken stones used for knapping points and other everyday tools, and he loved constantly finding connections to the present. Every moment was a lesson, every day a chapter in my learning.

My father's time would not be long, and in his passing I knew he had given me the tools I needed for the road ahead. I took my father's advice to seek out his clan relatives for assistance whenever I needed it. Shortly after becoming the first woman director of Acoma's Historic Preservation Office, I met with my father's clan relative, T'sachiya, whom I referred to as uncle. Not only did he resemble my father but he spoke in many ways like him. I was fortunate to have him as a member of my advisory board and was able to spend days with him in the field working on various projects—and, as my father had

Figure 11.2. Kaweshtiima (Mount Taylor) after the first winter snow. Courtesy of Theresa Pasqual, photographer.

Figure 11.3. The Acoma Pueblo Valley, looking south, with the village visible in the distance. Courtesy of Theresa Pasqual, photographer.

urged, returning to the places of our collective past. It was on an outing to Chaco Culture National Historical Park that he put our connection to the San Juan region into perspective for me:

> S'amaak'u [daughter], this place belongs to you. It is a part of who you are. All the places to the north, Kuutsisruma; all those places that take us to the days past are in you. Our Acoma people and the people that lived in these places were related, they knew of each other. They had their own journey, our path brought us here. Look and you will see.

With that I revisited many well-known sites, including Aztec, as well as sites off the beaten path, taking my time to get reacquainted, as if seeing a long-lost family member. I introduced myself in the appropriate traditional way and asked the sprits to teach me what they wanted me to know. Each place had a unique identity and sense of purpose; each place had a role to play and for certain amounts of time. These sacred places— Kuutsisruma—were as alive and well at the time that my own village and its surrounding settlements were built and occupied. As my father noted, these ancestral places, including Acoma, were ideal locations because of their proximity to water. Our own village was situated near multiple springs and had access to tinajas where water was collected and had abundant alluvial plains. Also, the Rio San Jose flows to the north of Acoma Valley, making it an ideal place for agriculture (fig. 11.3). The old people farmed much like my own father did: dry farming but also building by hand systems to divert water to lands suitable for growing the staples that would sustain a community and serve as commodities for trade.

The construction of the ancestral village was not random; as in my own village, the builders took note of the daily paths of the sun and moon on their journeys across the heavens. The integral relationship between human and universe reflected in purposely mindful construction that captured views of the horizon using natural features to mark their movements. The placement of ceremonial spaces was deliberate and a reflection of both the order and chaos of the heavens. Understanding the order and flow of things both natural and human-made allowed individuals to meet their responsibility toward keeping order and balance in the universe.

The collective knowledge passed down from our ancestors, to my people, my clans, and my own family influenced the construction of my mother's house. My father used this generational knowledge held by his father and elder male relatives to source and cut stone by hand. In order to learn it he had to participate in it, the same kind of transmission of knowledge and language that, according to my uncle, T'sachiya, took place in the past. Although work was done collectively in the days of Aztec and Chaco, individuality and creativeness still came through. For example, my father built in touches that made my mother's house unique, using local stones that contained fossils as a reminder of the ocean that was part of our world. The builders of Aztec were influenced by the builders of Chaco, but they also added their own unique touches, adding colored stones to interior walls and utilizing materials that were locally accessible, such as river cobblestones and dried mud bricks.

Daily life, much like our own at the pueblo, would have been filled with the tasks needed to ensure that the basic needs of the village were met. Water needed to be collected, firewood gathered, and food prepared for the day's meals. Everyone had a responsibility, no matter their age, and everyone was expected to contribute, thus ensuring survival and continuity. We can see the discipline and skill of the old people reflected in what remains: the handwoven willow baskets and the mats, pottery, and adornments.

The religious and political system of old was complex even in its newness. The stories of both my uncle and my father attest to the fact that Chaco served a distinct purpose in our evolution. It was a place where the connection to the elements and the ability to control them was strong, but however powerful it was, it was not sustainable. What flowed from Chaco to the places often referred to as outliers were the core values, the ideas old and new. It was this balance of old ways and new that moved people forward—to unfamiliar places of settlement and to integrating these ways of thinking into villages that were already occupied.

There is strength in Pueblo thinking, a comforting continuity that comes from a constant return to the core values—love, respect, stewardship, honor—that have guided us since the time of emergence. It is easy to lose this perspective on the people who once lived when we only look at their places analytically. I needed twenty-five years to understand my place in the Puebloan continuum. By standing in the river, by experiencing these places in quietness, by remembering and praying, I can connect to my relatives, my ancestors, in the present moment. Their knowledge continues to shape our world through the lessons that my father and uncle continue to teach me even in their absence. As stewards of these special places, we can protect and preserve them, ensuring that the river of our past continues to flow and that the stories and songs, the wisdom of those past, are ever present and alive.

Suggested Reading

A large body of literature exists on the archaeology of the Middle San Juan, Chaco Canyon, and greater Mesa Verde regions. Here we offer a few suggestions of recent work.

Brown, Gary M., Paul F. Reed, and Donna M. Glowacki
2013   "Chacoan and Post-Chaco Occupations in the Middle San Juan Region: Changes in Settlement and Population." *Kiva* 78:1–31.

Fagan, Brian
2005   *Chaco Canyon: Archaeologists Explore the Lives of an Ancient Society*. Oxford, UK: Oxford University Press.

Heitman, Carrie C., and Stephen Plog (editors)
2015   *Chaco Revisited: New Research on the Prehistory of Chaco Canyon, New Mexico*. Tucson: University of Arizona Press.

Kohler, Timothy A., Mark D. Varien, and Aaron M. Wright (editors)
2012   *Leaving Mesa Verde: Peril and Change in the Thirteenth-Century Southwest*. Tucson: University of Arizona Press.

Lekson, Stephen H.
2015   *The Chaco Meridian: One Thousand Years of Political and Religious Power in the Ancient Southwest*. 2nd ed. Lanham, MD: Rowman & Littlefield.

Lekson, Stephen H. (editor)
2006   *The Archaeology of Chaco Canyon*. Santa Fe, NM: SAR Press.

Lister, Robert H., and Florence C. Lister
1987   *Aztec Ruins on the Animas: Excavated, Preserved, and Interpreted*. Albuquerque: University of New Mexico Press.

Noble, David Grant (editor)
2004   *In Search of Chaco: New Approaches to an Archaeological Enigma*. Santa Fe, NM: SAR Press.
2006   *The Mesa Verde World: Explorations in Ancestral Pueblo Archaeology*. Santa Fe, NM: SAR Press.

Reed, Paul F. (author)
2004   *The Puebloan Society of Chaco Canyon*. Westport, CT: Greenwood Press.

Reed, Paul F. (editor)
2006   *Thirty-Five Years of Archaeological Research at Salmon Ruins, New Mexico*. Tucson, AZ, and Bloomfield, NM: Center for Desert Archaeology.
2008   *Chaco's Northern Prodigies: Salmon, Aztec, and the Ascendancy of the Middle San Juan Region after AD 1100*. Salt Lake City: University of Utah Press.
2011   "Chacoan Immigration or Local Emulation of the Chacoan System?" Special issue, *Kiva* 77 (2).

Contributors

LARRY L. BAKER has served as the executive director of the San Juan County Archaeological Research Center and Library at Salmon Ruins for twenty-four years. He has more than forty years of experience as a professional archaeologist in the northern Southwest, specializing in analyses of prehistoric and historic architecture and the preservation and stabilization of these structures.

GARY M. BROWN is an archaeologist and cultural resource manager with the National Park Service. His first major excavation project was at Salmon Ruins in 1976 under Dr. Cynthia Irwin-Williams. He came full circle in 2000 when he began work at Aztec Ruins National Monument after many years of work throughout the Southwest. Along with several authors in this volume, he was a key member of the Middle San Juan Project, which laid the groundwork for much of this book.

KATHY ROLER DURAND is professor and chair of the Department of Anthropology and Applied Archaeology at Eastern New Mexico University. She specializes in the analysis of animal and human bones recovered from archaeological excavations. Her current research focuses on the study of animal bones from Aztec, Guadalupe, and Salmon Ruins, New Mexico, and the exploration of changes in diet and ritual practices in these prehistoric communities.

FLORENCE C. LISTER's career in archaeology began in 1940, when she attended the University of New Mexico field school in Chaco Canyon. She and her husband, Robert "Bob" Lister, conducted archaeological projects in northern and central Mexico, Africa, and the southwestern United States. She authored or coauthored forty-eight published works based on her research. Florence died at her home in Mancos, Colorado, on September 4, 2016.

ETHAN ORTEGA is a lifelong New Mexico resident. He earned a BS in anthropology from Eastern New Mexico

University and currently works for New Mexico Historic Sites, specializing in research, interpretation, and exhibits. His goal is to make the archaeological collections of New Mexico more accessible to the public and researchers alike.

THERESA PASQUAL of Acoma Pueblo is the former director of the Acoma Historic Preservation Office. Her current work focuses on the protection of cultural and archaeological resources of tribes in the Southwest.

LORI STEPHENS REED is an archaeologist at Aztec Ruins National Monument. She has an MA in anthropology from New Mexico State University and has spent most of her career studying pottery of the Southwest.

PAUL F. REED lives in Taos, New Mexico, and is a preservation archaeologist with Tucson, Arizona–based Archaeology Southwest. He has worked as a Chaco scholar at Salmon Ruins, New Mexico, for sixteen years. Reed is editor of *Chaco's Northern Prodigies: Salmon, Aztec, and the Ascendancy of the Middle San Juan Region after AD 1100* (2008) and *Thirty-Five Years of Archaeological Research at Salmon Ruins, New Mexico* (2006).

H. WOLCOTT TOLL has worked in Colorado and New Mexico archaeology since 1972, when he began work with Dr. David Breternitz. His 1985 University of Colorado PhD dissertation was based on work with the National Park Service Chaco Project, and he took a job with the Museum of New Mexico Office of Archaeological Studies when an opportunity to work in La Plata Valley arose. The large volume of data from that project has been the main focus of his twenty-nine years with the Museum of New Mexico.

MARK D. VARIEN currently serves as the executive vice president of the Research Institute at the Crow Canyon Archaeological Center in Cortez, Colorado. In this position he works with his colleagues to further the center's three-part mission: to increase knowledge of the human experience through archaeological research, to conduct that research in the context of public-education programs, and to partner with American Indians on the design and delivery of those research and education programs.

LAURIE D. WEBSTER is an anthropologist and independent scholar who specializes in the textile traditions of the American Southwest. She is a visiting scholar in the School of Anthropology at the University of Arizona and a research associate at the American Museum of Natural History in New York and the Crow Canyon Archaeological Center in Colorado. Her publications include the edited volume *Beyond Cloth and Cordage: Archaeological Textile Research in the Americas* (University of Utah Press, 2000) and the book *Collecting the Weaver's Art: The William Claflin Collection of Southwestern Textiles* (Peabody Museum Press, 2003). She lives in Mancos, Colorado.

Index

Page numbers in italic text indicate illustrations.

Pueblo Bonito, xiii, 1–2, 24–25, 44, 47–48, 69, 74–78, 80, 84–86, *85*, 90

Pueblo people, xiii, xiv, 3, 4, 10, 15, 23, 25, 27–28, 31, 34, 46–51, 53, 57–58, 62–63, 65, 67, 69, 71, 73, 80–81, 89, 93, 95–96, 99

rabbits: cottontail, 63–65, 67; jackrabbits, 64–65, 67

Reed, Lori S., xi, 11, 74, 81, *83*, *85*, 86, 87

Reed, Paul F., ix, 1, *1–2*, 21, 71, 82, 93

Rio Grande, xiv, 10, 44, 71, 73, 96

ritual, xiv, 4, 6, 8, 10, 20, 23, 24, 48, 50–51, 53, 57, 60, 62, 71, 73, 78–79, 84–86, 93. *See also* ceremonial

roads, Chacoan, 5, 7, 20, 36

Rocky Mountains, 3, 31

Salmon Pueblo, xiii, xiv, 1–2, 6, 7–10, *8*, 21–29, *21*, *22*, *24*, *25*, *26*, *27*, *28*, 35, 42, 55, *55*, 56, 57, *57*, 66–71, *66*, *67*, 69, 74, 76–77, 84, 86

Salmon Ruins, xi, xiv, 4, 29, 53, 54, 105, 107; Museum, xi, *8*, *22*, *23*, *24*, *25*, *26*, 27, 29, 54–56, *57*, *66*, *67*, 69, *70*, 86

San Juan Basin, xiii, xiv, 3, 36–37, 45, 53, 90

San Juan College, 84

San Juan County Museum Association, 27, 29, 55

San Juan period, 22, 63, 66;

San Juan River, xiii, 3, 9, 21–23, *21*, 25, 28, 45, 53, 84, 99

San Juan Valley Archaeological Program (the Salmon Project), xi

San Mateo site, 99

School for Advanced Research, ix, xi

Southwest (region), 3, 5, 8, 25–26, 28, 42, 45, 52, 62–63, 65, 69–71, 73, 78, 80–82, 93

Spanish explorers/travelers, xiv, 27, 31, 71, 82

St. Johns Polychrome pottery, 84, 87

summer solstice, 3, 34, 53–54, 56–58, *59*, 68

Taos, New Mexico, 70

Teague, Lynn, 29

Tewa language, 96

Texas, 96

Tiwa language, 96

Toll, H. Wolcott, 10, *18*

Tommy site, 66, 71

Totah, ix, 13

Towa language, 96

Tower kiva at Salmon, 24, *24*, 26, 27, 54–55, 68

tree-ring dates, xiv, 7, 8, 15, 42, 44, 61

tri-wall structure, xiv, 40, 58, 60, 93

turkeys, 15, 63, 66, *66*, 68, 70, *70*; burial of, 25, 70; feathers, 71, 73, 77, 79

turquoise, 18, 24

Tuzigoot National Monument, 51

Twin Angel pueblo, 1, *1*, 2

University of Colorado Museum of Natural History, *39*, *46*, *49*

University of New Mexico Press, ix

Utah, 19, 74, 79, 97

Varien, Mark, 11, 89

Village Ecodynamics Project (VEP), *90–92*, *92–93*, 98

Webster, Laurie, xi, 11, 71, 73, 74, *76–79*

West Ruin of Aztec, xiv, 57–58, 74, 76, 77, 78, 79, *83*, 87. *See also* Aztec: West

White Mountain Red Ware pottery, 84

Wilhusen, Richard, *91*

winter solstice, 3, 34, 53–54, 57–58, *59*

Wupatki, 51

Zuni, Pueblo of, 10, 34, 84; language, 96